BOUNDLESS
COMPASSION

"If it can be said that *Praying Your Goodbyes* is Joyce Rupp's most memorable book, then I believe that *Boundless Compassion* will turn out to be her signature generative work. In it she begins by sharing a simple, life-changing event for her. Then, as we read further, we are given the chance to transform as well. We learn how with true compassion realism meets hope; we are invited to sit with other wisdom figures whose words she includes in her text; and we are given the rare opportunity to personally experience a retreat—which this book really is—with one of today's leading spiritual midwives. *Boundless Compassion* calls us to be compassionate to others and to ourselves in the richest way possible, with Jesus Christ as our ultimate model. Why not respond to this call by slowly enjoying the companionship of this extraordinary book? It may turn out to be the most significant prayer experience you have this year or for years to come."

Robert J. Wicks
Author of *Riding the Dragon*

"Joyce Rupp's *Boundless Compassion* is a subversive book promoting a subversive practice. Compassion shatters the twin idols of nihilism and narcissism in which we take refuge from both the awesome and the awful that is our everyday reality. This book shows you how to live lovingly with both without making a god of either."

Rabbi Rami Shapiro
Author of *Perennial Wisdom for the Spiritually Independent*

"Transformative Joyce Rupp presents us with a practical, no-nonsense invitation and challenge to change ourselves and our world by becoming, and living out, compassion. This book will both inspire us and deepen us into God."

Edwina Gateley
Poet, author, and speaker

"The Gospels are insistent: be compassionate. But they do not tell us how to get there. We need Joyce Rupp for that. She gives us a program and a process on how to develop a compassionate consciousness and find the behaviors that embody it. My guess is that if you engage these reflections and exercises, a new courage will rise in you and the path of compassion will open before you. But the proof is in this very excellent pudding. Taste it."

John Shea
Author of *Seeing Haloes*

BOUNDLESS
COMPASSION

Creating a Way of Life

JOYCE RUPP

SORIN BOOKS  Notre Dame, IN

© 2018 by Joyce Rupp

www.sorinbooks.com

Paperback: ISBN-13 978-1-932057-14-0

E-book: ISBN-13 978-1-932057-15-7

Cover image © Kirstin McKee/ Stocksy.com.

Cover and text design by Brian C. Conley.

Printed and bound in the United States of America

Library of Congress Cataloging-in-Publication Data is available.

To Margaret Stratman, O.S.M., colleague and friend, whose wisdom and guidance companioned my every step from the earliest birthing of Boundless Compassion,

and to each participant of the Boundless Compassion workshops, retreats, and conferences. Their insights and experiences energized the contents of this book.

CONTENTS

TRODUCTION

Compassion asks us to go where it hurts, to enter places of pain, to share in brokenness, fear, confusion, and anguish. Compassion challenges us to cry out with those in misery, to mourn with those who are lonely, to weep with those in tears. Compassion requires us to be weak with the weak, vulnerable with the vulnerable, and powerless with the powerless. Compassion means full immersion in the condition of being human.

—Donald McNeill, Douglas Morrison,
and Henri Nouwen, *Compassion*[1]

Thirteen years ago I stood at the patio door of my kitchen with the deepest sorrow burrowing into my heart. Five hours earlier one of my dearest friends had died of a brain hemorrhage. I was trying to absorb this enormous loss when a hummingbird fluttered in front of my face, just a few inches outside the glass. It hovered there, facing me for several minutes, enough time to convince me that my friend—who treasured those little creatures—was assuring me all would be well. As the tiny bird departed, an inner knowing swept through my being: "Love is all that counts." Since that moment I have never been the same.

Because my selfless friend exuded compassionate presence, I had little doubt that message was intended for me. I turned from the patio door determined to give the rest of my life to living in such a way that compassion would be the most essential focus. Three years later I came across a magazine ad that directed my life completely toward that commitment. I noticed that His Holiness the Dalai Lama was scheduled to lead a conference on teaching families how to be compassionate. I have long admired this Tibetan Buddhist leader and what he teaches. This admiration began when I lived in Boulder, Colorado, while attending Naropa, a Buddhist university, during graduate studies. While there, I grew in admiration for Buddhism's dedication to compassion. I left there newly inspired, determined to incorporate this central feature of the world's major religions more fully into my Christian life.

As I read the description about the Dalai Lama's workshop, I thought, *I really appreciate his wisdom. I wonder who is teaching Christians how to be compassionate?* And thus began the greatest challenge and joy of my life: developing and teaching the Boundless Compassion program. Sr. Margaret Stratman, also a Servant of Mary, joined me in consulting a variety of persons in caring professions in an effort to gather pertinent information for the program's content and to create a viable structure that would encourage participants to live compassionately. After a year-long consultation we shaped the Boundless Compassion program, offering it as either a four-day conference or a retreat. The 1,200 participants repeatedly confirm the program's value by assuring us, "Taking part in this study of compassion has changed my life."

In codirecting the program I recognize that the desire to live compassionately requires constant learning and personal renewal. As Christina Feldman writes in *Compassion: Listening to the Cries of the World*, "We are always beginners in the art of compassion. No matter how advanced or refined we believe our understanding to be, life is sure to present us with some new experience or encounter with pain we feel unprepared for. . . . Over and over you are asked to meet change, loss, injustice, and over and over you are asked to find the strength to open when you are more inclined to shut down."[2]

There is nothing wimpy or starry-eyed about this essential Christian virtue. Living compassionately is rarely convenient and often downright challenging. It requires a willingness to pay the price for being aware of suffering and doing what is possible to diminish it.

The call to compassion has been with me for a long time. A life-size replica of Michelangelo's *Pieta* rests in a large niche at the front of my religious community's chapel. Ever since my days as a young member, I have felt the call to accompany others in their suffering. When I gaze at the depiction of Mary sitting with the body of her executed son across her lap, I see a mother whose grief weighed like a boulder on her maternal heart. I long to receive those who suffer with the depth of Mary's loving presence.

Compassion thrived in the heart of Jesus and in his teachings. If there is one virtue that most exemplifies his life, it is this one. While I esteem the wisdom of various religious traditions that emphasize compassion in their principles, I most of all resonate with those of my beloved teacher, Jesus, a person of immense love. When Jesus urged his followers to be compassionate, he knew what he was asking. Everywhere he went his awareness of people's suffering became evident. He poured out his love and gave generously of his time, energy, and concern to relieve their pain of body, mind, and spirit.

Jesus also challenged those whose policies, regulations, and personal behavior caused or contributed to suffering. As his voice for justice gained strength, so did the voices of those who wanted him destroyed. Jesus knew both the risk and the price to be paid for being committed to compassion. In *A Spirituality of Caregiving*, Henri Nouwen recognizes this challenge: "The Gospel call to be compassionate is one that goes right against the grain, that turns us completely around and requires a total conversion of heart and mind. It is indeed a radical call, a call that goes to the roots of our lives."[3]

While many Christians have yet to grasp the full significance of a total dedication to compassion, we have an exemplary leader and witness of this commitment in the spirituality of Pope Francis. His courageous teachings and humble actions reveal compassion as a way of life, an inner posture of mind and heart, one meant to infuse our whole being. The following words of Pope Francis demonstrate how his compassionate approach establishes itself in a strong rootedness in following Jesus:

> This love [of God] has now been made visible and tangible in Jesus' entire life. His person is nothing but love, a love given gratuitously. The relationships he forms with the people who approach him manifest something entirely unique and unrepeatable. The signs he works, especially in favor of sinners, the poor, the marginalized, the sick, and the suffering, are all meant to teach mercy. . . . Nothing in him is devoid of compassion.[4]

This book is not about easy answers; nor does it suggest that we can "fix" the world's suffering or eliminate it entirely from those closest to us. Rather, *Boundless Compassion* extends an invitation to grow in the kind of love that motivated Jesus to be a compassionate presence. This love will then flow generously through us into the lives of those who ache for a touch of loving-kindness. Each of the six weeks' material presents insights and examples of how to enter into situations that contain travail and difficulty. This requires being in touch with how we think, feel, and respond to the suffering residing in ourselves and others, and how we interact with the extensive differences that trouble our world.

My friend Kathy commented one day that there is a big difference between a nudge and a shove. A nudge moves us toward growth. A shove initiates resistance. *Boundless Compassion* is meant to nudge, encourage, and inspire each reader to be a beloved, Christlike presence. Being "a living Christ" today compels us to embody compassion as he did, to ease suffering, to welcome and aid those who are most vulnerable, and to toil for justice in a global society that wields the heavy weight of domination and oppression.

The greatest challenge of compassion may well be that of recognizing the dignity and worth of every person—regardless of race, gender, culture, creed, political stance, or personal behavior. The light of divinity dwells within each one, no matter how hidden that goodness might be. South African archbishop Desmond Tutu often speaks and writes about the power that this belief can have on how we live:

> We are fundamentally good. When you come to think of it, that's who we are at our core. . . . What difference does goodness make? Goodness changes everything. . . . Goodness changes how we see the world, the way we see others, and most importantly, the way we see ourselves. The way we see ourselves matters. It affects how we treat people. It affects the quality of life for each and all of us. What is the quality of life

> on our planet? It is nothing more than the sum total
> of our daily interactions. Each kindness enhances the
> quality of life. Each cruelty diminishes it.[5]

In today's society it often seems as if cruelty is more extensive than kindness.

Broken, wounded, violent, damaged, divisive—these are some descriptions given to the current global situation. Our world desperately needs the noble, essential quality of compassion to be activated—and will not heal without it. Depending on how we respond, we can increase or decrease the amount of anguish in our world. Only with compassion at the core of humanity's lived experience will we be able to approach one another with true respect and dwell in peacefulness.

$\mathcal{S}$UGGESTIONS FOR USING THIS BOOK

The use of *Boundless Compassion* depends on what best assists the reader in enriching an understanding of this most basic and essential human attribute. My goal is that each reader will be reinspired and motivated to live compassionately. Some may find the essays sufficient for their interest. Others may wish to include a more in-depth and integrated method of using this resource. It is to these readers that I suggest the following.

INDIVIDUAL STUDY

You will need to set aside at least twenty minutes to focus on the theme and content for each day. A question for reflection follows each day's content. Before responding to the question, pray for guidance and insight. Welcome silence, and allow the question to take up residence within you. When a response arrives, write this in a notebook or journal, so you can look back at the end of the week and recall what emerged for you. A brief prayer follows each reflection. Lastly, a scripture verse awaits for you to tuck in your heart, if you so choose. This serves as a reminder to animate a particular aspect of compassion throughout the day.

The seventh day of each week consists of a review, to recall what you have integrated during the week. This is not a time for assessing "how you performed." Rather, it is an opportunity to pause and remember what you discovered or relearned about compassion. This review helps you recognize what stirred and called to you and where it led you in the growth of compassion. This is a day for gratitude and rest.

GROUP STUDY

Group gatherings strengthen the study of compassion by kinship—joining in a "common cause" and sharing the enriching benefit of one another's insights after a week of study. When each week is completed, the following design for the group's gathering could be used:

- Begin with an opening prayer or meditation from *Prayers of Boundless Compassion.**

- Discuss the past week, using the questions for Day 7.

- Have quiet time to allow the richness of the sharing to be absorbed.

- Check to see if there is any further input from anyone in the group.

- Conclude with a prayer from *Prayers of Boundless Compassion.*

*Prayers of Boundless Compassion is an available companion resource, containing prayers and meditations related to the topics

for each of the six weeks in *Boundless Compassion* (Sorin Books, www.avemariapress.com).

CIRCLES OF COMPASSION

After a retreat or conference on compassion, participants are encouraged to form a Circle of Compassion to keep both their continued learning and their practice of compassion alive. This is something you might wish to do after completing *Boundless Compassion*. These Circles nurture the bond of kinship among those who value compassion. They also provide encouragement to embody compassion by a study of resources and the sharing of personal experiences in living compassionately. Circles meet once a month for two hours. The following format is one that has evolved and is now used by past participants of the Boundless Compassion retreats and conferences:

- Opening meditation of ten minutes. The form of this to be decided by the Circle. Meditations from *Prayers for Boundless Compassion* could be used.

- Personal sharing in groups not larger than three. Five minutes is allotted for each person. The sharing is based on this question: "How have I experienced, or not experienced, compassion during the past month?" Application of listening skills and compassionate presence are essential for this sharing. (This is a "faith sharing" time, not a counseling or therapeutic session.) The content of the small group is confidential and is not brought to the large group.

- Discussion of a resource related to the topic of compassion is then held for the remaining time.

- Close with a blessing or prayer led by the facilitator of the Circle.

Compassion as a Way of Life

INTRODUCTION

*The joys and hopes, the sorrows and anxieties of the
women and men of this age, especially the poor and
those afflicted in any way, are the joys and hopes, the
sorrows and anxieties of the followers of Jesus Christ.*

—Vatican II, *Gaudium et Spes*[1]

In my early twenties, the first line of this Vatican II document on the Church, *Gaudium et Spes* (Latin for "Joy and Hope"), aroused a vision in my heart of how I wanted to live. Ever since then, this hope has formed a motivation for my steadfast longing to respond compassionately to those whose lives bear "sorrows and anxieties," to bring joy and hope to "those afflicted in any way."

Paul Gilbert, professor at Derby University, describes compassion as "being sensitive to the suffering of self and others with a deep commitment to try to prevent or relieve it."[2] This week we explore some of the basic components of doing this. I invite you to consider what compassion consists of in its most basic nature. This includes exploring the movement of compassion—*awareness, attitude, action*—and the four essential aspects of *nonjudgment, nonviolence, forgiveness,* and *mindfulness.*

Compassion is a way of life—an inner posture of how to be with suffering, both our own and others, and a desire to move that attitude into action. Compassion involves an "inside-out" movement. A radical change unfolds in us when compassion becomes a way of life, a transformation as far-reaching as an acorn growing into a tree, an egg producing a chicken, or a caterpillar metamorphosing into a butterfly.

Each of the practices of compassion presented this week holds the possibility of changing how we think, how we respond emotionally, and what choices we make in regard to others and our planet. We cannot accomplish this transformation on our own. Only with divine love empowering us and a daily renewal of intention will we be insistent and persistent in our efforts to live in a compassionate manner.

My experience with compassion has taught me that activating this virtue is both a challenge and an immense gift. I know that my intent to be compassionate has changed me. I have become more generous with my presence, less begrudging of the time required to be there for another. Negative criticism and judgment of others has waned considerably, and in their place has grown a greater acceptance and appreciation for those who think and act differently than I do. My understanding of the pain that our planet and nonhumans endure steadily expands. At the same time, I am always learning more about what compassion requires.

One of the ongoing strengths of compassion rests on the foundation of our unity with this world of which we are a part. We are never alone in our practice of compassion. At the same time, we continually receive what we need to sustain our life and our love. As meditation teacher Norman Fischer reminds us:

> Literally every thought in our minds, every emotion that we feel, every word that comes out of our mouth, every material sustenance that we need to get through the day, comes through the kindness of and the interaction with others. And not only other people but nonhumans, too, literally the whole of the earth, the soil, the sky, the trees, the air we breathe, the water we drink. We not only depend on all of this, we are all of it and it is us.[3]

Keeping this bountiful support in view helps us to meet the challenges that compassion brings with it.

Each day that we give ourselves to living compassionately, we will need a trustful patience. With the exception of biologists and a few other interested human beings, most of us never pay attention to photosynthesis, that phenomenal gift of the sun to change light into food. This process takes time. Plants do not grow into full stature overnight. Some, like trees, take years to reach their full height and fruitfulness. Matt Malone, S.J., editor in chief of *America* magazine, alludes to this reality by relating the story of Hubert Lyautey, who "once suggested to his gardener that he plant a tree. The gardener objected, 'This particular tree will not flower for a hundred years.' To this the former French Army general replied, 'In that case, plant it this afternoon.'"[4]

We presume that we must wait for a tree to grow. This is true also with our desire to be persons who contribute to a lessening of the world's suffering. Compassion is the photosynthesis of the heart. It too requires the slow, trusting process of waiting for change to occur. We cannot hurry this transformation, but we can give ourselves to it as fully as possible, knowing that it entails a continual recommitment.

Mindfulness is a valuable means of maintaining and strengthening our resolve to begin anew each day. Day 6 presents the value of this spiritual practice to keep us alert so that we are aware of suffering and how we choose to respond to it. As you reflect on the topics of this week, be patient with yourself. Trust that you have a divine companion who both inspires and guides you along the way.

WEEK 1, DAY 1

AWARENESS, ATTITUDE, ACTION

*Compassion is a thread that binds together the
deepest centers of life beyond the borders
of race, gender, religion, tribe, or creature.*

—Ilia Delio, O.S.F., *Compassion*[5]

Awareness. Attitude. Action. These three essentials comprise the movement of compassion. While much of the world's suffering is observable, a portion lies tightly concealed. Unless we become *aware* of suffering, we cannot respond to it compassionately.

One day in a supermarket I met an acquaintance whom I rarely see. She smiled and commented on life "being good" in reply to my "how are you?" Three minutes into our conversation, her tears fell as she spoke about the helplessness of seeing her parents aging. Another time, at Mass on a Lenten morning, a stranger in a business suit sat next to me, seemingly content, until a cell phone behind us rang incessantly. The man turned around and hissed, "Throw the damn thing out the door!" Only at the Sign of Peace did I catch a glimpse of what disturbed his spirit. A woman came over to him and whispered, "Good luck on your deposition today." Ah, there it was—the hidden anxiety and concern about what lay ahead of him.

Compassion also requires a certain *attitude*, that of recognizing the inviolable oneness we have with all of life. We exist in a world of interconnectedness. We are not isolated individuals, even if we may feel that way at times. The suffering of one affects the suffering of all. What we think and feel about people who are suffering, especially if they do not match our notions of how they ought to believe and act, greatly affects our response.

The indwelling light of divinity unites us at a spiritual level. If I intend to be compassionate, I cannot shove people I dislike out of the way. I relearned this one morning sitting in prayer at dawn, watching charcoal clouds press heavily against the eastern horizon. In spite of this barrier, a strong, thin edge of brilliant red light arose. This persistent light led me inward to where disgust toward a political leader lodged. His hard-hearted approach to society's most vulnerable people walled off my thinking kindly about him.

As I observed the narrow band of light, I remembered Jessica Powers's poem about the Holy One "sitting on a ledge of light" in her soul.[6] With that, the Spirit of Love opened my walled-off heart, and I thought, *This politician, too, has a ledge of light in his heart, even though I cannot see it. Soften what has concretized in yourself.* This insight did not mean accepting his noncompassionate rhetoric and heartless actions, but it did call me to look beneath that behavior and respect the Light at the core of his being.

Later that morning I received confirmation of my insight when I opened Krista Tippett's *Becoming Wise* and read a comment by Congressman John Lewis of Georgia:

> You have to be taught the way of peace, the way of love, the way of nonviolence. In the religious sense, in the moral sense, you can say that in the bosom of every human being, there is a spark of the divine. So you don't have a right as a human to abuse that spark of the divine in your fellow human being. . . . If you have someone attacking you, beating you, spitting on you, you have to think of that person. Years ago that person was an innocent child, an innocent little baby. What happened? Did something go wrong? Did someone teach that person to hate, to abuse others? You try to appeal to the goodness of every human

being and you don't give up. You never give up on anyone.[7]

Research by quantum physicists like David Bohm assures us that we are also united on a physical plane by a bond of invisible connections. Our physical self consists of invisible energy packets of light and heat called photons. Instead of our bodies being a solid mass, scientists now know that every particle is in motion. Each part connects and interrelates with each other. Lynne McTaggart summarizes this research in *The Bond*: "The more scientists look, the more they discover how dependent on, and finally indivisible from, everything is with everything else."[8] We are beings who intermingle in an undetectable way with one another. Amazing indeed.

This attitude of a common bond underlies each compassionate *action*. With our awareness of suffering, and an attitude of wanting to alleviate it, we then choose to act in a positive way for the benefit of all beings. We trust that each action taken for the good of one person or group benefits the good of all—that, as we read in *Gaudium et Spes*, "the sorrows and anxieties of the women and men of this age . . . are the sorrows and anxieties of the followers of Jesus Christ."[9]

This three-step approach can clearly be seen when Jesus approaches the widow of Nain (see Lk 7:11–17). He becomes aware of her suffering when he sees her crying at the death of her son: "He had compassion for her and said to her, 'Do not weep'" (Lk 7:13). His heart is moved because he recognizes a human being like himself who knows loss and sorrow. This elicits loving-kindness in him and a desire to end her suffering. Jesus then acts by raising the son back to life.

We look beneath surface appearances when we are compassionate. Like Congressman Lewis, we trust the spark of divinity dwelling in humanity. On the surface we may seem to exist at a

great distance from each other. Underneath that cover of disparity lies the treasure of our oneness. The deeper down we go, the
more alike we are than different. Each of us desires happiness.
Each of us knows fear and the pain of nonacceptance. Each of us
wants to have a loving home in the heart of another. In the wise
words of conservationist Carl Safina, "The greatest story is that
all of life is one."[10]

REFLECTION

Of the three components of compassion—awareness, attitude,
action—which do you find most difficult to live? What makes
this challenging for you? How might you approach this so that
it becomes less difficult?

PRAYER

Imagine that a ledge of light exists in the vast abode of yourself.
You are sitting on that ledge. An embodied, compassionate presence comes and joins you. As the two of you sit together, on each
in-breath whisper quietly: "I am filled with compassion."

SCRIPTURE TO CARRY IN YOUR HEART TODAY

"Clothe yourselves with compassion" (Col 3:12).

WEEK 1, DAY 2

THE SEEDS OF COMPASSION

What we repeatedly think shapes our world. Out of
compassion, substitute healthy thoughts for unhealthy ones.
—Jack Kornfield, *The Wise Heart*[11]

At the opening of a retreat on compassion, I handed each participant a small transparent pouch containing four seeds. I reminded them that the seemingly inert seeds held the potential
for an abundant harvest if they were carefully tended. I asked
the group to consider the seeds as symbols of the four main spiritual qualities necessary for compassion's growth: *nonjudgment,*
nonviolence, forgiveness, and *mindfulness.*

The more these seeds are nurtured, the greater the harvest
of compassion. Enlivening these four aspects requires deliberate practice, interior stamina, and trust in the power of the Holy
One to assist in their development. When we look into the gospels, it doesn't take long to find numerous teachings of Jesus
related to these qualities: "Do not judge, so that you may not
be judged" (Mt 7:1). "[Forgive] not seven times, but . . . seventy-seven times" (Mt 18:22). "If anyone strikes you on the cheek,
offer the other also" (Lk 6:29). "Keep awake" (Mk 13:35).

Neuroscience lends credence to both the challenge and the
possibility of bringing these seeds to life. We now know that
every human being is born with the potential for being compassionate. Sometimes severe psychological trauma in early
childhood damages this ability to sense the suffering of others,
but for the majority of people this seed waits to be generative.
Authors such as Paul Gilbert, Rick Hanson, and Daniel Siegel,

MD, have explored the connection between the brain and its ability to activate compassion. Gilbert writes:

> Understanding our minds is perhaps one of the greatest challenges for modern science and each of us personally. . . . It's our minds that will create grasping selfishness, pitting group against group, or an open, reflective, cooperative, and sharing approach to these difficulties. And, of course, it is our minds that are the source of our own personal experiences of happiness and joy, or anxiety, misery, and despair.[12]

Neuroscientists once thought that brain cells lost an ability to adapt once a person reached a certain age. Now they teach the theory of *neuroplasticity*, which assures the possibility of brain cells changing throughout our lifetime. Research in the area of meditation, for example, has found that neurons, or nerve cells, in the part of the brain affected by meditation are much thicker and stronger for those who meditate daily for lengthy periods.

Any thought or action we do repeatedly will strengthen that part of the brain, as Daniel Siegel notes in *Mindsight*: "One of the key practical lessons of modern neuroscience is that the power to direct our attention has within it the power to shape our brain's firing patterns, as well as the power to shape the architecture of the brain itself."[13] A common saying among neuroscientists when they speak of this is, "Neurons that fire together wire together." The more that nerve cells transmit information through electrical and chemical signals called synapses, the sturdier those areas of the brain become.[14]

We are capable of changing what we think and how we respond. The more intentionally we concentrate on being nonjudgmental, nonviolent, and forgiving, the stronger our possibility of being able to respond that way becomes. For instance, if I am having difficulty in trying to be less judgmental about someone, I can reduce that negativity by consciously intending to notice my thoughts about that person, and then choosing to alter them if they are not kind. As I do so repeatedly, the neurons in that area of my brain gain strength in their ability to be less judgmental. Awareness of my thoughts increases, and I am more conscious of where I let those thoughts lead me.

I know this is possible from personal experience. In my youth I observed how adults I admired dealt with difficult relationships by using "the scissors method." Instead of entering into dialogue when conflicts arose, they simply cut off the lines of communication by their silence, or by completely ending the relationship. Snip. Snip. Snip. No more connection. So, of course, this is what I did until young adulthood when I realized this approach strongly opposes what Jesus taught. Slowly, by staying with the intention of moving away from negative thoughts and from my desire to snip off a relationship, I went toward dialogue and communication. It took quite a few years before those neurons in my brain strengthened enough to support my ability in handling relationship conflicts differently.

We plant the seeds of compassion by being aware of our thoughts and feelings, and by the deliberate intention to think and respond in a kindhearted manner. In *The Compassionate Mind*, Paul Gilbert affirms this possibility of changing our brain: "So what you focus on, aspire to, and *practice* will make a difference to your brain and that is true for compassion training, too."[15] In other words, we can teach our minds to activate compassion, so that we do not react on impulse, or go about our lives unconsciously, missing opportunities to alleviate suffering—and create more suffering.

What do you do with your thoughts and feelings? Do they run rampant all day without being tended? Do they move your heart toward loving-kindness? The qualities of nonjudgment, nonviolence, forgiveness, and mindfulness wait to be nurtured. I invite you to focus on each of these during the rest of this week.

REFLECTION

If you have access to four seeds, use them to represent the four seeds of compassion. If not, cut four small pieces of paper. Write the name of one of the seeds of compassion on each paper. Choose one of these, and put it in the palm of your right hand. Place your left hand on top of it, as if covering a seed in the soil. As you breathe in, breathe this quality of life into your heart. Do this for two or three minutes. Then repeat the gestures with the other three seeds, or words. Put these in a place where you will see them the rest of the week, to remind you to nurture these qualities within you.

PRAYER

Gardener of My Inner Being, you enrich the soil of my heart with your bountiful love. I will do my part each day to grow seeds of compassion in that soil.

SCRIPTURE TO CARRY IN YOUR HEART TODAY

"The one who sows sparingly will also reap sparingly, and the one who sows bountifully will also reap bountifully" (2 Cor 9:6).

WEEK 1, DAY 3

BEHIND EVERY SCAR, A STORY

*Compassion can never coexist with judgment because
judgment creates distance and distinction, which
prevents us from really being with the other.*

—Henri Nouwen, *The Way of the Heart*[16]

While sitting beside the Des Moines River one day, I wrote the following in my journal: "A turkey vulture, a blue heron, and a bald eagle have flown past me this morning. Words flit through my mind with every sighting, giving each bird a value and a status, all according to my small mind—*don't like, love it, thrilled at, repugnant, strong, scary, beautiful.* I do the same with people. Label, label. label."

We all need to make choices and decisions that affect our lives. However, when we compare our values, beliefs, and opinions to how others ought to look, speak, and act—and become critical when they do not meet our criteria—judgment becomes divisive and noncompassionate. How quickly we can get caught in comparing and categorizing others according to our biases. This negative valuing adds to, rather than lessens, individual and global suffering. Harsh judgment keeps love at a distance and blocks peace.

I heard Fr. Joseph Nassal, author of *The Conspiracy of Compassion*, comment in a presentation, "We always see through the lens of our own experience." He then asked his audience to let their relationships with others be influenced by the reality that "behind every scar there is a story."[17] People believe and behave the way they do because of their personal history and the hurts they have experienced. We do not know people's stories, their condition of body, mind, and spirit. Nor do we know their motivations. We may think we know someone well, but there is much that is unknown to us.

We can be quick to evaluate people in the way I judged the birds. A participant in a Boundless Compassion retreat once told of recognizing this condition in herself. "Anne" was visiting in a large city and stood on a crowded corner waiting for the light to change. Across the street from her, she noticed a man who "looked evil" by her standards—"dirty beard, body covered with tattoos, unkempt clothes." She immediately became afraid of him. When the light changed, a car came flying down the street and went through the red light. At that moment, she saw "the evil man" instantly put his arm out in front of a blind woman next to him as she started to cross the street. His quick response saved her life. Needless to say, Anne's harsh judgment about this man immediately changed.

Self-righteousness smugly decides whether someone is worthy of compassion. Fr. George Smiga points out that Jesus began with compassion, not judgment, when he fed the five thousand: "He could have begun differently. He could have stepped off the boat and said, 'Look at all these spiritually dead people. Why don't they take responsibility for their lives? Why don't they spend more time in the temple or studying God's law? How can they come out to a deserted place without food? They do not even have the sense to carry a lunch with them!'"[18]

An insight of Rabbi Michael Paley provides a way to pull back judgment of others. In reflecting on Moses's only being allowed to see God's back when what he really wanted to see was God's face, Paley comments: "In our relationships with other people, we often ask to see their faces but maybe we should ask to see their backs so that we can see the world, maybe only for an instant, the way they see it. Then we can offer them true understanding—a genuine gift."[19]

I recalled Paley's suggestion when I heard National Public Radio's host Krista Tippett speak at Drake University. I left there with valuable insights from her. Among them is that, when we are with someone whose vision differs significantly from our own, we should ask the question of this person: "Where does it hurt?" I wish I had thought of that before I grew progressively irritated with the coordinator of a large event where I was scheduled to speak. It seemed to me that he was overly controlling and trying to make certain my presentation would reflect his ideas, not mine. When I complained about this to a good friend, she remarked, "It sounds like he must be very worried about the conference." That simple comment immediately freed me to look at the issue by standing at the back of the coordinator and seeing it from his eyes: *What was his concern, his hurt?* When I thought about that, my irritation left, and peacefulness took over.

After Timothy McVeigh was sentenced to death, he answered the question, "Are you sorry for killing all those people, especially the sixteen little children, when you bombed the Oklahoma City federal building?" McVeigh answered coldheartedly, "Everybody's grandmother and kids die. Get over it." At first I loathed him for that response. This changed after I thought about how barnacled his heart had become, like an impenetrable stone. Then I could move toward compassion for him. I felt sadness for a human being who was that completely alienated from love. I grieved for the seed of goodness that lay inert in the dark soil of his heart, buried beneath fabricated perceptions and hateful illusions.

Compassion insists that we look "on the heart" the way the Holy One does: "The LORD does not see as mortals see; they look on the outward appearance, but the LORD looks on the heart" (1 Sam 16:7). Instead of critically name-calling and voicing disgust or hate, we remember the core of goodness residing in each individual, no matter how suppressed that goodness might be.

REFLECTION

Call to mind someone whom you judge disapprovingly, or someone whom you wish to change in order to meet your criteria. Imagine you are standing behind that person's back, looking out through his or her eyes. Ask yourself where this person might be hurting.

PRAYER

Merciful One, you look into the heart and see what we mortals cannot see. Pull me away from making disparaging judgments. Move me toward greater compassion for those whose appearance and behavior differ from mine.

SCRIPTURE TO CARRY IN YOUR HEART TODAY

"Do not judge, and you will not be judged" (Lk 6:37).

WEEK 1, DAY 4

RESPONDING NONVIOLENTLY

*Our capacity to be a cause for suffering and our
capacity to end suffering live side by side within us.*
—Christina Feldman, *Compassion*[20]

How is it that a person can be warmhearted in one instance and hard-hearted the next? I learned this can happen in less than a minute. One early winter morning I was calmly driving to our women's prayer group. The sun had not yet risen, and snow on the roadside stood so high that vehicles barely had room to navigate on the two-lane street. My sleepy mind quickly awakened when headlights came directly toward my car as I drove down a steep hill. I had nowhere to turn and feared a direct hit. In the nick of time, the oncoming pickup moved back over to the other lane. I looked to see that the driver had passed a bicyclist. Immediately my calm self filled with anger: *Stupid person putting us all in danger!* More nasty epithets rushed into my mind. Soon, I was wishing the driver harm: *Maybe he or she will have a flat tire. I hope the police issue a ticket.*

Then a stronger message arrived: *Look, you're going to a* prayer *group. Do you want to carry this energy there?* That was when I remembered compassion. My mind turned toward the driver of the truck. My heart began sending forth peace. I did not know if impatience, lack of attention, or something else caused the near collision. What I did know was that I could stop the negativity in myself. I continued to wish the driver well, and by the time I walked into the prayer group, my angry response had dissolved. If I had not been attentive to what was happening interiorly, I would have carried that vengeful energy to the group, and soon we would all have been talking about "that idiot driver."

Marianne Williamson refers to this attentiveness in *Illuminata*. She points out that "the source of violence is in our heads. As it would not be appropriate to ignore 'just a little' cancer in the body, so it is not appropriate for us to ignore 'just a little' violent thinking. A little cancer, unchecked, turns into a monstrous killer. So do small, insidious, seemingly harmless judgmental thought forms become the pervasive cancers that threaten to destroy a society."[21]

Every human brain contains an instinctual realm that responds to fear. This part of us (known as the amygdala) developed in early humanity's brain when tribalism existed. In order to survive, the people needed to protect themselves from marauders out to destroy their tribe and steal their life-giving resources. This resulted in aggressively defending themselves from those outside their tight circle of existence. Their brains developed fast-responding triggers to keep them from being harmed.

While this part of the brain often protects us, it also sparks hatred, greed, and self-orientation. Think how subtly this happens in our society when personal space appears threatened: "Don't cut into my line of traffic." "You took my seat." "Don't step on my lawn." "You barged in front of me." "Don't shove your truth into my religion or politics." "Stay away from my neighborhood." "You can't participate in our church service."

The instinctual part of my brain initially responded to the careless driver by alerting me to possible injury when he came toward my side of the street. I instantly felt scared. I wanted to flee, get out of the way, but after that, I wanted to "fight," to hurt the "invader." Today we have a much more developed brain, an outer layer known as the neocortex whose frontal lobe gives us the ability to pause, think, reflect, and then make a decision about how to act. It keeps us from going about our lives mindlessly, from acting on impulse and lashing out. Fortunately, the frontal lobe of my neocortex enabled me to let go of my anger-laden name-calling and to reflect on a more appropriate response, one that lessened my hostility.

When we follow our negative impulses without taking time to reflect, we easily move toward destructive reactions in various ways. Intentionally damaging words can verbally slap a person and make them feel smaller or discounted. Retaliatory desires create a faceless adversary: "I hope he gets the electric chair." "She had it coming to her." "Kick them out of the country." "I bet he fails miserably." "Give them what they deserve." "Maybe she'll lose her job." "Serves him right for lying." Careless comments contain damaging words: "Kill 'em with kindness." "I could have beat her." "They shot down his suggestion."

"It hit him between the eyes." "That report knocked her off her high horse." Enforced silence reflects another form of violence. Refusing to speak cuts off the possibility of reconciling communication with another; it depersonalizes and denies the right to be heard. Imposed silence slams the door shut on relationships. Certain physical gestures depict hostility such as raising a middle finger, lifting an eyebrow, grimacing, or having an intimidating glare or a smirk.

Mahatma Gandhi gave his life to nonviolence as a way to bring about justice. He defined this peaceable approach as "avoiding injury to anything on earth, in thought, word, or deed." He believed that "nonviolence is the greatest and most active force in the world."[22] Martin Luther King Jr. expressed something similar when he spoke of nonviolence as not only avoiding physical violence but avoiding violence of one's spirit, as well. An example King gave was that of refusing to shoot a person and also refusing to hate that person.

To be nonviolent indicates that our mind and heart are open to others. Hatred and revenge have no place in anyone, especially those who follow the teachings of Jesus. Could "love your enemies and pray for those who persecute you" (Mt 5:44) be any clearer? If we are to live compassionately, then nonviolence will encompass both our inner and outer life.

REFLECTION

Look back on the past several days. When did the instinctual part of your brain take over and lead you to respond with some form of violence (with thoughts, words, silence, or actions)? You might want to have a conversation with this part of your brain to see how your future responses could be different.

PRAYER

Place your hands on your forehead; set an intention to send forth kind thoughts instead of reactionary ones when you are upset. Place your hands on your heart; set an intention to be a person with an inner peace that calms and keeps you from responding violently.

SCRIPTURE TO CARRY IN YOUR HEART TODAY

"Then Jesus said to Peter, 'Put your sword back into its place; for all who take the sword will perish by the sword'" (Mt 26:52).

WEEK 1, DAY 5

FORGIVENESS IS A JOURNEY

And Blackness stretched forth the rough hand
to the white hand
and cherished it into the clearing.
This Blackness forgave what it would not forget.
And marched on remarkable feet.

—Gwendolyn Brooks, "In Montgomery"[23]

We do not forget. Our mind has a file of memories that refuse to be deleted. Poet Gwendolyn Brooks reminds us of this. Black people who endured the despicable reality of slavery could not forget that white owners stole their life and liberty. Instead, in a remarkable gesture of love, blacks chose to stretch out a hand to whites. This did not happen in a day or a year, and it still continues today, with whites slowly reaching back.

Pardoning one another takes time. As Jean Vanier notes: "Forgiveness is a journey, it is not just an event."[24] When Jesus said we are to forgive seventy-seven times (see Mt 18:22), he indicated that this gesture of our will involves a process, not a one-time occurrence. We may need to forgive the same person or situation over and over because memories of that grievance keep popping into our consciousness like pottery shards showing up in an archaeological site. These memories generate emotions that shut out the desire to forgive. Even so, we continue in our efforts to let go until the memory visits us less often and loses its potency. Eventually those memories no longer exert power over us.

In the 2016 film *Manchester by the Sea*, Lee is a young father whose carelessness after carousing with male friends costs the lives of his three young children. Because of heavy drinking and drugs, he accidentally sets the house on fire in which the children lie sleeping. Throughout the film we see how Lee cannot forgive himself for causing this tragedy. Sadness, grief, and guilt obliterate his joy as he clutches self-inflicted anger to his wounded heart. This leads to a projection of his anger onto others—lashing out verbally, starting physical fights, and becoming a recalcitrant loner. When his wife Randi, who divorced him after the accident, realizes the agony Lee continues to go through, she approaches him and asks forgiveness for the horrible things she said to him after the fire. Lee turns away without accepting her invitation to lessen the grief he carries, choosing to continue to punish himself with guilt. He remains unable to release the relentless burden of self-reproach.

The Lee and Randi story reminds me of Jack Kornfield's description of forgiveness in *A Path with Heart*: "Forgiveness is simply an act of the heart, a movement to let go of the pain, the resentment, the outrage that you have carried as a burden for so long. It is an easing of your own heart and an acknowledgment that, no matter how strongly you may condemn and have suffered from the evil deeds of another, you will not put another human being out of your heart."[25] Keeping another person in our heart does not eliminate the necessary justice for a crime committed or other injurious actions. We also need to protect ourselves from harm and set boundaries to safeguard against being used or abused by others. Nor does forgiveness mean we have to reestablish a relationship. Forgiveness *does* imply that we do not seek revenge. We pray for peace to be with all those involved, and we do what is possible for that peace to evolve.

When we cannot give and receive forgiveness, a part of us gradually becomes a remote island. Compassion slowly turns away, hiding out under the rock of a hardened heart. In *Manchester by the Sea*, Randi tended her justified outrage. As she did so, her heart opened compassionately toward Lee. But Lee could not do the same with his sorrowful regret. Had he chosen to offer compassionate forgiveness to himself, he could have begun the healing process. Instead, the searing pain remained within him.

While compassion loses its ability to alleviate or end suffering when we refuse to forgive, it gains strength when we pardon others for their wrongdoings. Mark Nepo verifies this in a true story about forgiveness. Don and his wife were heading home after shopping for groceries when a truck driver, partially blinded by the late-day sun, was fiddling with the radio to find a music station. At that moment, the truck driver swerved and broadsided the car, causing it to burst into flames. Don's wife, in her early thirties, died in that crash, and he sustained serious burns. Many years later, Don, now in his seventies, was driving past a fruit stand when the memory of that terrible accident came back to him with all its pain. The remembrance reappeared so strongly after all those years that he stopped his car and cried. That's when he decided to find the truck driver.

Although it took a while, Don located the man and extended an invitation to have coffee at a local shop. When they met, Don soon realized that the man still carried guilt and regret for what he had caused to happen. As Don watched the truck driver's discomfort, he took his hand and managed to get out the words, "I forgive you." At that point, the truck driver broke down and told Don he had never driven a truck since the accident. Later, when Don spoke about that encounter, he explained why he made the effort to meet the person whose action caused him so much grief: "I just had to let the man off the hook."[26]

In Nepo's story we see compassion and forgiveness woven together. Don's empathy helped him get past his sorrowful memory. The gesture of kindness to someone who hurt him allowed that painful experience from the past to lose its strength. At the same time Don's compassion freed the truck driver from suffering the weight of his regretful deed.

When we forgive, we lift encumbrances from our own heart and another's as well. This allows space in us for greater love, and an easing of hurt that might have interfered with our compassion for a lifetime. It takes a magnanimous person to keep letting go until the heart grows free enough to forgive, free enough to fully love, free enough to be compassionate.

REFLECTION

What do you believe about forgiveness? What would you say to someone who asks you what is needed in order to forgive?

PRAYER

"We have a ritual once a year where everyone goes down to the water's edge and we throw water over our back seven times. In that moment we are washing away those thoughts and actions that we recognize as no longer necessary or beneficial for our continued growth" (Dhyani Ywahoo, *Voices of Our Ancestors*).[27]

Merciful One, open my mind and heart so that I recognize and remove any nonforgiveness that continues to dwell there.

SCRIPTURE TO CARRY IN YOUR HEART TODAY

"Put away from you all bitterness and wrath and anger and wrangling and slander, together with all malice, and be kind to one another, tenderhearted, forgiving one another, as God in Christ has forgiven you" (Eph 4:31–32).

WEEK 1, DAY 6

STAYING AWAKE

*We have seeds of compassion, understanding, and love
in us. We all have many good seeds of happiness and
joy. Yet we also have the habit of running in us. This
restless energy of dissatisfaction and struggle
separates us from the present moment and from ourselves.*

—Thich Nhat Hanh,
"Watering the Seeds of Happiness"[28]

In order for compassion to be more than a distant ideal, a mechanical gesture, or an action done out of duty and guilt, we will need to be faithful to a daily spiritual practice. This helps to clear our spirit of whatever distracts or impedes our compassionate presence. Much has been written about the value of "mindfulness." This ability to stay awake to what goes on within and outside of us is absolutely necessary for compassion.

Paul Gilbert explains how awareness is helpful in this regard: "Compassion helps us reorganize our minds by generating particular motives and feelings, while mindfulness helps us step back and disengage from emotional thinking loops that suck us in, hereby providing the stability and perspective which is the basis for insight."[29] In other words, mindfulness helps us assess whether our thoughts and feelings are pulling us toward or away from compassion.

When I first learned about mindfulness, I thought it to be about noticing details and actions of my external world. That type of awareness is definitely a part of mindfulness. Alertness to the "here and now" readies us for a much deeper and more extensive type of being present to what's around us. Then, being aware externally opens our consciousness and strengthens our ability to look within to notice what is occurring interiorly.

When I am "mindful," I avoid getting caught by what insists on claiming my mental or emotional attention, such as judgmental thoughts or unkind feelings. One of my first experiences of living mindfully on an interior level happened years ago when I traveled to visit friends in Colorado. I stopped at a rest area, and when I walked into the building, I noticed a volunteer behind the information counter. I needed a map, so I went over and politely asked the man if he had any available. To my surprise, he snapped at me in a gruff voice, "Well, if you'd open your eyes, you'd see they're right in front of you." Instantly, I felt irritated and disliked the man. I wanted to rebuff him with a nasty response such as, "Well, with an attitude like that, you shouldn't be working here." Instead, I swallowed my words and left to take my lunch from the car and sit at a picnic table.

As I sat there, I wanted to keep the past alive by repeatedly reviewing the scene and holding a grudge against the man. Instead, I paused to breathe slowly. This took me away from the past and into the present moment. I became conscious that my brain's instinctual response wanted to get back at the man's curt-ness by using some angry words to get even. I then pondered the situation with the gift of my neocortex's frontal lobe. I considered what might have caused the man to speak that way. Perhaps he was a new widower, or he suffered from severe chronic pain, or maybe he developed an angry personality from family history. This process of paying attention to my interior responses, and then choosing to act in an appropriate manner, awakened my better self and released my hostility. By the time I had finished lunch, I no longer thought or felt any need for harboring verbal retaliation. I wanted the man to be peaceful and happy. And I was peaceful and happy, too.

Day 2 included the research of neuroscientists who assure us that the more we practice thinking and acting in a certain way, the stronger those particular neurons in our brain grow. This is especially significant for mindfulness practice. We need to attend to awareness constantly, as mindfulness teacher Jon Kabat Zinn states: "You may have to remember over and over again to be awake and aware."[30] Meditation, journaling, daily discernment, pausing, breathing—all these practices help me to be mindful, and in turn they help me to be more compassionate-ly responsive.

Mindfulness is not only about focusing on negative, or dis-tressful, interior responses. It is foremost about becoming aware of how we experience life, moment to moment. We are so easily absorbed in the endless "do this now" details of life, and in in-formation overload, that our awareness acquires a clouded win-dow. Paul Gilbert suggests that as we learn to pay attention, we will develop our ability to "refocus our attention to appreciate and savor things." We will be more "curious about our feelings rather than . . . frightened of them or in denial about them; and, most of all, [we will learn] how to be kind—which lies at the heart of compassion."[31]

Centering prayer as taught by Fr. Thomas Keating and other contemplative leaders assists in the practice of mindfulness and, ultimately, compassion. This form of meditation serves to free us from the constrictions of our limited views and behavior, from the ceaseless flow of external activity, and from the continual interior discourse that tries to claim our total attention. Centering prayer also animates our relationship to the Holy One. It reanchors our mind and heart in the gospel teachings, all of which connect us to compassion.

Cynthia Bourgeault's reference to centering prayer as "a methodology par excellence for nurturing the heart" applies equally to the ability of mindfulness.[32] Both forms of practice draw us into the embrace of compassion and strengthen the positive manner in which we activate it.

An adapted form of a prayer that St. Ignatius taught can be especially helpful in establishing the discipline of mindfulness. This practice of daily discernment involves pausing for a few minutes several times during the day to visit the sanctuary of our inner being. In this reflective space, we review our interior movements and discern how we are experiencing them: *What am I thinking? How am I feeling? What has the quality of my response been to those interior movements? Has this put me in touch (or out of touch) with divine compassion?*

Sometimes my reflection involves a realignment of attitude or behavior, becoming conscious again of needing to act with loving-kindness. At other times, my answer to these questions fills me with gratitude for my positive attentiveness.

REFLECTION

"Compassionate abiding, like sacred holding, is a practice that encourages us to 'go within before venturing out.' If we are able to go *within* with what we find difficult or dislike, we are less likely to react impulsively when we *venture out* and more likely to respond compassionately" (Diane M. Millis, *Conversation — The Sacred Art*).[33]

What usually keeps you from being mindful? How is your practice becoming more attentive?

PRAYER

Beloved Presence, awaken my mind when it roams incessantly and forgets about coming home. Awaken my heart when distractions disturb and pull me away from equanimity. Call me home each time I wander away from the present moment. Help me remember where I am and who you are.

SCRIPTURE TO CARRY IN YOUR HEART TODAY

"What I say to you I say to all: Keep awake" (Mk 13:37).

WEEK 1, DAY 7

REVIEW AND REST

Compassion is a heart-to-heart encounter because compassion flows from the human heart; it is not a rational conclusion to a problem. Rather, it is an act of love beyond what the mind can comprehend. The heart therefore must be able to see what may be blind to the physical eye.

—Ilia Delio, O.S.F., *Compassion*[34]

Choose any or all of the following as a way to review Week One:

• What three aspects of "Compassion as a Way of Life" were of greatest significance to you this past week?

• As this first week ends, what are your thoughts and feelings regarding the activation of compassion in your life?

• How does the content of Week One connect with your experience of the spiritual life?

• Which day's reflection challenged you the most?

• Which one left you nodding your head yes?

• As you look back over the week, were there moments or situations that awakened your compassion?

• Draw a "Tree of Compassion."

   ♦ *Roots*: Your life experiences that provide a strong foundation for the practice of compassion.

   ♦ *Trunk*: Personal qualities and characteristics that enable you to be a conduit of compassion.

- *Branches*: Situations and circumstances that challenge you to reach out with compassion.

- *Leaves*: Ways in which you have received compassion.

- *Fruit*: Specific ways you have offered compassion to self and others.

WEEK TWO

WELCOMING OURSELVES

INTRODUCTION

*I could never extend a boundless compassion
to anyone unless I know deeply what it means
to hold myself in a compassionate heart.*

—Christina Feldman, *Compassion*[1]

When Jesus referred to the second great commandment, "Love your neighbor as yourself" (Mt 22:39), he could have reworded it: "Be as welcoming of yourself as you are welcoming of your neighbor." *When is the last time you fully welcomed yourself into your own heart?* Most of us hesitate to do this.

Some people overdo it by extreme self-orientation or narcissism. Having self-compassion does not mean self-absorption. "This kind of compulsive concern with 'I, me, and mine' isn't the same as loving ourselves," writes Sharon Salzberg. "Loving ourselves points us to capacities of resilience, compassion, and understanding within that are simply part of being alive."[2]

Self-compassion implies giving ourselves a worthy share of attentive care. This includes body, mind, and spirit—and all the "to do" items that self-help advocates suggest for leading a balanced and wholesome life: getting enough sleep and exercise, eating healthily, taking time for leisure, developing social relationships, and having a spiritual practice. However, these restorative measures are only part of the nature of self-compassion.

Self-compassion also includes being kind and comforting to ourselves when we are hurting. In addition, it involves how we view who we are, the judgments we make in regard to our self when we are stressed, overworked, experiencing failure, and when life does not proceed the way we planned. Self-compassion means staying with our self in times of trouble, pain, and grief.

Kristin Neff points to this in *Self-Compassion*: "Self-kindness involves more than merely stopping self-judgment. It involves *actively* comforting ourselves, responding just as we would to a dear friend in need. It means we allow ourselves to be emotionally moved by our own pain. . . . With self-kindness, we soothe and calm our troubled minds. We make a peace offering of warmth, gentleness and sympathy *from* ourselves *to* ourselves, so that true healing can occur."[3]

People who faithfully offer compassion to others often neglect to do the same for themselves. This truth revisited me on the morning I chose to play Libby Roderick's song "How Could Anyone" for Dana, a woman struggling with her worthiness. As Dana listened to the song about believing and trusting in one's inner beauty, tears streamed down her cheeks. When the song ended, she marveled, "I've often played that song for women in the prison, but I never thought of playing it for myself."

Besides leaving ourselves out of the kindness we give others, we also expect a lot of ourselves, expectations that prevent self-compassion. We drag ourselves to work when our bodies feel miserable. We push on to attend a social gathering even though it would be better for us to stay home. We feel deep sadness but shove it aside, saying, *I shouldn't hurt this much*, or *I ought to be over this by now*, or *I don't have time to think about this*. If we are ill, how many of us say to ourselves, *I'm really sorry you're feeling this way; I'll take good care of you*? Most often, we just suffer through the flu or a chronic illness, maybe even blaming ourselves for not feeling well. And if we pray for others, do we also pray for ourselves?

Any and all of the following require our compassionate care: our less than perfect self; external, difficult events and experiences that cause us stress, sorrow, and suffering; inner turmoil and struggles that only we know; difficulties with relationships; thoughts and feelings we wish we did not have; our own and others' expectations of us; difficult issues that go back to early childhood; acceptance of our physical appearance and how the body changes and ages.

If we have compassion for our self, we will continually become a healing presence for others without saying a word or doing anything extraordinary. We will convey kindness by our presence, by our attitude toward their suffering and our own. Christina Feldman explains it this way:

> Exploring your inner world, the relationships you form with all that arises in your body, heart, and mind, you discover a microscopic view of the relationship you form with all of life. Within this inner world, you sow the seeds of the compassionate heart or the alienated heart. In your relationship to your pain and sorrow, you cultivate the patience, forgiveness, and understanding that inform your relationship with all pain and sorrow. It would be naïve to believe that profound compassion could be found to meet the great sorrow in life if you do not hold yourself in the same light. The training ground of boundless compassion is in all the small moments in which you meet the painful and difficult within your own life that you are prone to deny or reject.[4]

A fundamental truth rests beneath the practice of self-compassion: We are good. We are worthy of consideration and comfort. We deserve our own respect. Jesus was speaking to every person when he taught, "I came that they may have life, and have it abundantly" (Jn 10:10).[5] If we are worn to a frazzle, depleted of hope, or nit-picking at our faults and imperfections, we will not have the receptivity required to embrace this bounty.

WEEK 2, DAY 1

BREATHING IN AND OUT

We feel the rhythm of compassion moving in and out,
connecting us to the eternal rhythm of life.

—Gail Straub, *The Rhythm of Compassion*[6]

Try this: Take as deep a breath as you can. Now, let it out as fully as possible. Keep pushing your breath out until you absolutely cannot do it for one more second.

Notice how you ached to inhale that next breath?

We need the balance of inhaling and exhaling. Gail Straub uses this image in *The Rhythm of Compassion* to demonstrate the two sides of compassion. "Breathing in" represents caring for self, and "breathing out" signifies compassion for others.[7] Pope Francis uses another metaphor: the systolic and diastolic beating of the heart, the blood flowing in the heart and moving out.[8] Our bodies cannot survive without these natural rhythms. Neither can our inner life. Yet, there is a strong tendency in many compassionate people to breathe out, out, out, and to neglect the precious in-breath.

Our American culture does not encourage breathing in. Rather, it pushes us toward constant activity and gauges our worth by how busy we are. This attitude affects everyone, but it especially applies to people in service professions and those whose lives involve full-time caregiving. They focus their attention on "breathing out," disregarding their own needs, even when they feel exhausted and increasingly overwhelmed. Wendi Steines understands this. She said, "The hardest part is getting myself to *breathe* some days." In her forties, Steines is the divorced mother of fourteen-year-old Nicholas and eleven-year-old Adam. Both

children have autism spectrum disorder, along with other be-
havioral syndromes. No wonder she finds it challenging to take
an in-breath.[9]

Christopher Germer emphasizes how important self-care is
if we are going to generate genuine compassion for another. In
The Mindful Path to Self-Compassion, he describes a situation with
his wife when he planned to be her caregiver. The first morning after she came home from having hip surgery, he was determined to help her out. She is a morning person; he is not. But he
got up anyway, convinced he could offer the essential assistance
they previously decided she would need after surgery. Germer
looked forward to the opportunity to show his affection for his
wife. But soon he felt tense and grumpy as he tried to put on her
pressure-sock sleeves. By the time he tried getting shoes on her
swollen feet, he began secretly to blame her for his having to get
up early, but at the same time he was concerned that his wife
might think she was asking too much of him.

Finally, Germer became aware of the problem. He has hy-
poglycemia and had not had anything to eat or drink before he
began helping his wife. Once he paused to have some orange
juice, he felt much better and managed to assist her with ease
and confidence. Had Germer first taken care of his own need, the
tussle and negativity he experienced would not have happened.
They both would have been happier.[10]

For several years, I searched for an image to represent
self-compassion. I finally found it in the dawn when I stood by
my cousin's patio door, gazing sleepily at a thick blue spruce
tree. A winter storm had left the tree densely suffused with snow.
All of a sudden, I thought I saw movement deep in the branches.
I looked more closely and caught a wondrous sight. Two tiny
black eyes peeked out at me from within the spruce. A dove sat
there with feathers fully fluffed to keep itself warm. The bird
looked like a chubby, white snowball. I couldn't help but smile,

thinking of the dove's wisdom—hiding in the tree and knowing the fluffed feathers would act as insulation from the freezing air.

After that morning, I became intrigued with how birds care for themselves. I always thought preening their feathers was simply an act to entice a mate. Well, it *is* that. But preening is so much more. After seeing the dove in the spruce tree, I carefully observed pelicans, herons, geese, loons, and other wildfowl preen themselves. I studied and learned that birds must groom or lose their ability to fly and navigate in water. Preening involves layering feathers so birds have balance in flight, pulling out the tattered ones, picking off parasites and lice that carry disease, and removing tough feathers so newer ones have room to grow. The birds also take oil from the base of their feathers and spread it onto them so they will be waterproof.

Like birds caring for their feathers, we must also groom our "feathers"—layering our activities and putting them in proper order so our lives stay balanced. We preen our thoughts and feelings, ridding them of the parasites of self-criticism and harsh judgments, pulling out the mind-sets that keep us from being kind to ourselves, and oiling our positive qualities with consistent practice. With this preening, we allow ourselves to become more loving and positive in our outlook. We discover what artist Rita Loyd did when she reflected on self-love: "If you feel like something is missing from your life, know that often what is missing is you—a fully alive you—a fully satisfied you, with all parts of you activated and awake."[11]

Be good to yourself today. Become more fully alive, awake, and satisfied. And don't forget to do some preening.

REFLECTION

What part of your life needs some preening? How might you go about doing this?

PRAYER

Breath of Life, you are with me; I am with you.

I breathe your love into my heart.

I breathe this love out to the world.

SCRIPTURE TO CARRY IN YOUR HEART TODAY

"For we are the temple of the living God; as God said, 'I will live in them and walk among them'" (2 Cor 6:16).

WEEK 2, DAY 2

THE SELF-COMPASSION OF JESUS

Jesus seems to have taken every opportunity of getting away to a quiet and lonely place for prayer and reflection.

—Albert Nolan, *Jesus Today*[12]

A minister met with me to discern her future. After an extensive conversation in which we explored her situation, I suggested she gaze deeply within herself and ask: "What do I need to be happy?" Her face lit up with joy as she told me what this might be, but that elation lasted briefly, followed by the objection, "Oh, no, that's quite selfish. I'd have to ask another question."

Is the desire to have a way of life that brings satisfaction a selfish choice? This pastor thought so. I disagree. The problem with the minister's thinking is that it not only denies God's natural gift of joy, but it also sets in motion the probability of compassion fatigue. Ordained clergy speak to their congregations about sacrificing for the sake of another and encourage other-centeredness. How many clergypeople address the topic of self-compassion, being attentive and kind to one's self? Probably not many. This may be due to clergy and other church personnel's inclination to avoid their own self-compassion. They work long hours, extend unmitigated service, give away their day off to tend to pastoral tragedies, and gradually come to believe their presence to be indispensable, convinced they are meant to give their lives totally, as Jesus did.

It is no wonder that this thinking exists. Consider some of Christianity's messages: "Give up your life for another." "Put others before yourself." "Give and do not count the cost." "It's better to give than to receive." These are not "bad" messages. Indeed, they reflect a significant part of the gospel teachings. Jesus "walked his talk." He lived those teachings by generously giving of himself, readily receiving those who came for healing, mercy, and encouragement. Yet, these messages and actions do not contain the whole story. What we infrequently hear is that Jesus also took care of himself. Look within the gospels to find evidence of this vital part of his life and ministry.

Early in Mark's account of Jesus, the disciple gives a vivid picture of his teacher's extensive and exhausting compassion (see Mk 1:29–35). Mark is impressed with how much Jesus did, telling us this in six short verses. Jesus first goes to Peter's ill mother-in-law and heals her from a life-threatening fever. That same day, in the evening, people brought all those who were physically, emotionally, and mentally ill. ("All" indicates a lot of people.) Not only does Jesus have these sick brought to him, but the press of the entire town collected at the door. Mark notes that Jesus "cured many" that night. How physically and psychically depleting an evening it must have been for him.

Mark is equally impressed with how Jesus takes care of himself by letting his readers know what happened after that energy-draining event: "In the morning, while it was still very dark,

[Jesus] got up and went out to a deserted place, and there he prayed." Jesus must have longed for an entire day to recover, but soon Simon and his companions "hunted for him." They invaded his solitude and hurried him from it, saying, "Everyone is searching for you" (Mk 1:35–37). Simon obviously did not recognize Jesus' need for physical and spiritual restoration. All that mattered to Simon was that Jesus meet the needs of others. Yet, time and again, the gospels mention Jesus going apart for renewal. He valued this kindness to himself. He respected his life, caring for and nurturing both body and spirit.[13]

The passage from Mark's gospel reminds me of my nephew's wife when their four children were young. Molly would lock herself in the bathroom in order to get a few brief moments of time by herself. The children pursued her, peeking under the bathroom door, insisting she come out. Jesus must have felt like that when his disciples hunted for him and urged a return to the crowds who begged for his presence. I've felt like that when my schedule is overloaded and another phone call comes asking me to do one more thing.

Numerous other gospel accounts offer glimmers of Jesus' self-compassion. He pauses during the day, "tired out by his journey," and sits down by a well (Jn 4:6). He recognizes the need for boundaries, giving himself some physical space in order not to be so pressed by the crowds. When Mary anoints his feet with precious oil, Jesus receives this gracious gesture of loving-kindness without objection. We see in his relationship with Mary, Martha, and Lazarus that Jesus knew how friendship strengthens a person's well-being. He is not about "all work and no play," but he takes time for social events such as the wedding at Cana. When his beloved friend Lazarus dies, Jesus allows himself to feel the extent of this loss.

Jesus is self-compassionate when he protects himself from harm by leaving places that reject him. When the local leaders are out to get him killed, Jesus knew this and "withdrew from that place" (Mt 12:15, NAB). When Jesus experiences the dread of future arrest and crucifixion, he longs to receive support from his disciples in his time of trial. He vulnerably asks them to be there for him in that frightening experience.[14]

From these illustrations of self-compassion, we see that Jesus obviously believed in people being attentive to their own needs. He never said, "You deserve this suffering." Instead, he lessened suffering in himself and others whenever possible. If we are to follow in his footsteps, we will give ourselves compassion as fully as we extend it to others.

REFLECTION

Which of the self-compassion experiences of Jesus especially relate to your life experience? If you were to write a letter to Jesus about self-compassion, what would that letter contain?

PRAYER

When my life becomes too crowded and I sorely need to pause and be renewed, remind me, Teacher of My Soul, how you rested and went apart from the pressures of your life. Grant me wisdom and courage to do the same.

SCRIPTURE TO CARRY IN YOUR HEART TODAY

"On that day, when evening had come, he said to them, 'Let us go across to the other side.' And leaving the crowd behind, they took him with them in the boat, just as he was" (Mk 4:35–36).

WEEK 2, DAY 3

APPRENTICE YOURSELF TO YOURSELF

Find that far inward symmetry
to all outward appearances, apprentice
yourself to yourself, begin to welcome back
all you sent away, be a new annunciation,
make yourself a door through which
to be hospitable, even to the stranger in you.

—David Whyte, "Coleman's Bed"[15]

The more we know and appreciate who we are, the more self-compassion grows. A lot depends on how we view ourselves—as Marianne Williamson shows in the following:

> There is a story about Leonardo da Vinci. . . . Early in his career he was painting a picture of Christ and found a beautiful young male to model for his portrait of Jesus. Many years later, Leonardo was painting a picture that included Judas. He walked through the streets of Florence looking for the perfect person to play the great betrayer. Finally he found someone dark-looking enough, evil-seeming enough to do the job. He went up to the man to approach him to do the modeling. The man looked at him and said, "You don't remember me, but I know you. Years ago, I was the model for your picture of Jesus."[16]

What do we perceive when we look honestly at ourselves? Do we recognize a friend? When we look in the mirror, do we see someone worthy of our acceptance and compassion? Do we believe we can learn from that person's wisdom, that we can be our own apprentice, as the poet David Whyte suggests?

Individual history and personality play a significant role in how we see ourselves and in how we approach our sufferings and failures. I did not grow up in a family that understood the value of self-compassion. Being of Germanic heritage, I learned to "tough it out," to not mention how or where I hurt. When I failed at doing something correctly, my father criticized me for it. I learned to hold back my tears, to swallow sorrow, and to believe I was less than worthy when I made mistakes.

A turning away from that misshapen attitude toward my hurts and limitations arrived in my midtwenties. When I learned of my brother's sudden death, a compassionate woman put her arms around me and whispered how sorry she felt. In that moment of comfort, the armor I had learned to place around my heart developed a crack. With future experiences of receiving consolation and kindly acceptance, the armor gradually decayed and fell away.

One of my friends experienced compassion in her family quite differently than I did. As a teenager she caused a minor accident on her first trip driving alone, hitting a parked car not far from her house. She walked home trembling in fear of a costly repair and severe reprimand from her father. She never forgot his surprising response: "Anybody can have an accident. What's important is that you are safe and no one was hurt. We can fix the car." This compassionate reaction opened the door for my friend to welcome herself with the same kindness as that given by her parent.

If we become aware of the messages in our family of origin, we are more prepared to offer self-compassion. With practice, we manage to shake off what keeps us from receiving kindheartedness from ourselves. In this spirit, a participant in one of our four-day conferences on Boundless Compassion wrote us to say,

"My cell phone fell into the toilet today. I tried not to listen to my old 'mother' message about being irresponsible."

Awareness of our personality type also lends helpful information about self-compassion. Continually placing impossible-to-meet expectations on ourselves does us a disservice. For example, if our personality type veers toward strong control, we may easily blame ourselves when things go awry. If we aim to please everyone in order to be liked, that will affect our kindness to self because we obviously cannot please everyone. If we are motivated by loyalty at all costs, we will sense defeat when others disappoint us no matter how superb our fealty.

Another participant in a Boundless Compassion retreat asked the question, "When is it self-compassion, and when does it become self-indulgence?" My response rested on how well we know ourselves: "Will this be helpful or harmful to my body, mind, or spirit, to my personal or societal relationships?" I recalled an experience of a pastor trying to serve three parishes at the same time. Few parishioners supported him. He would come home drained and discouraged from evening meetings. To ease his stress, he had an alcoholic drink. After a few months, each evening, he'd have a second drink. Then the night came when he thought he'd have a third. He paused and knew he was in trouble, realizing he could become totally reliant on alcohol. That evening he began total abstinence, and eventually he left the pastorate for another one that elicited his best gifts of pastoral leadership.

"By knowing yourself, you're coming to know humanness altogether. We are all up against these things." These comforting and compassionate words of American Buddhist nun Pema Chödrön remind us that we are not alone in the challenge to be self-compassionate.[17] The more we know and understand ourselves with our motivations, expectations, desires, and dreams, the healthier our self-compassion will be. When we give ourselves to this kindness, we also ripen our hearts to be kinder to others.

REFLECTION

How does your family history and personality influence your approach to self-compassion?

PRAYER

Creator of the Stars of Night, you formed the star of my own being in the dark months within my mother's womb. You have accompanied my every step since then, loving me as I am, providing for all that grows me into a golden soul of love. I thank you with all my heart.

SCRIPTURE TO CARRY IN YOUR HEART TODAY

"For it was you who formed my inward parts;

you knit me together in my mother's womb.

I praise you, for I am fearfully and wonderfully made.

Wonderful are your works;

that I know very well." (Ps 139:13–14)

WEEK 2, DAY 4

THE PROBLEM WITH PERFECTION

*We tend to treat ourselves with a level of harshness
and demand that we would be reluctant to inflict on
anyone else, even our worst enemies. Even as we open
our hearts to others, to receive and embrace them,
we habitually judge and condemn ourselves.*

—Christina Feldman, *Compassion*[18]

Yesterday the topic focused on friendship with our self. Now we look at another aspect of that friendship: acceptance of our *less-than-perfect* self. Our view of perfection can keep us from being self-compassionate. Pema Chödrön explains the consequences of this:

> Unconditional friendship with yourself has the same flavor as the deep friendships you have with others. You know yourself . . . you're kind to yourself. You even love yourself when you think you've blown it once again. . . . Repressing your tendencies, shaming yourself, calling yourself bad—these will never help you realize transformation.[19]

Self-loathing gets us nowhere, except to further dislike ourselves and move us even further away from spiritual growth. A young woman on retreat expressed dismay at a self-revelation: "I have discovered how strong my ego is. I can't stand myself. It's sickening to know how self-centered I am." I encouraged her to enter that awareness with less harshness and suggested she give herself support and understanding, to focus on gratitude for the graced awakening. When we become absorbed in nasty judgments and treat our limitations as an enemy, our energy escapes into a war with self. Consequently, we lose life-giving, growthful openness to the Holy One's transforming love.

It is an illusion to think we can get rid of everything we do not like or want to have in our personality. We *can* learn, however, how not to let these parts have power over us, not to act on them. In *Let Your Life Speak,* Parker Palmer explains how this self-acceptance can aid our spiritual growth:

> I now know myself to be a person with weakness and strength, liability and giftedness, darkness and light. I now know that to be whole means to reject none of it but to embrace all of it. . . . Others may say that "embracing one's wholeness" is just fancy talk for permission to sin, but again my experience is to the contrary. To embrace weakness, liability, and darkness as part of who I am gives that part less sway over me, because all it ever wanted was to be acknowledged as part of my whole self.[20]

Many people think the biblical text, "Be perfect, therefore, as your heavenly Father is perfect" (Mt 5:48), implies our having to become completely without blemish. Scripture scholars regard this translation as imprecise. The words "be perfect" actually translate as "be whole." Wholeness indicates a totality, as Palmer suggests. We are a combination of qualities. While we desire to live from our core goodness, we do not always do this. This humbling reality does not negate our essential worth. It does not make us "bad."

Brené Brown's book *The Gifts of Imperfection* offers beneficial insights about living from a sense of wholeness instead of a ruthless severity toward self. She suggests that we live "from a place of worthiness," that we cultivate "the courage, compassion, and connection to wake up in the morning and think, *No matter what gets done and how much is left undone, I am enough.* It's going to bed at night thinking, *Yes, I am imperfect and vulnerable and sometimes afraid, but that doesn't change the truth that I am also brave and worthy of love and belonging.*"[21]

Comparing ourselves to others often serves to intensify the way we disparage our lack of being perfect. "It usually means that you imagine the other person is better off, more satisfied—in a word, happier," writes Jesuit James Martin. He then answers the question of why we tend to do this: "Because we all know about our own problems, but other people's problems are harder to see. As a result, our real life always loses out."[22]

I find that I often need to reestablish my self-worthiness. One year when I spent three weeks at Rivendell Retreat Center in British Columbia, I overheard the staff refer to a population of weeds in the labyrinth. The next day I weeded feverishly during my breaks. After two days of tough work I learned that, instead of weeds, I was uprooting the Woolly Thyme they worked so hard to grow. (No wonder those "weeds" smelled so good.) I was embarrassed and apologetic, and I learned how wise it is to "ask first." At the same time, the kind manner in which the staff acknowledged my grievous error helped me to forgive my overly ambitious deed.

I remember an occasion when Linda, one of the members of our Circle of Compassion, adapted a reflective exercise from William Miller's book *Make Friends with Your Shadow* to teach us about acceptance of our whole self.[23] The exercise was particularly memorable. Linda asked each of us to spit into a small pill cup until it was about one-fourth full. We were aghast but went ahead with it. Then she asked us to look at our saliva (arrgh!), to touch it (more arrgh!), and finally to show it to our neighbor. After the exercise, Linda invited us to reflect on the value of saliva.

Without it our mouth becomes dry, and the lack of its vital enzymes prevents our food from being properly digested.

So, as much as we thought spittle to be obnoxious, we learned its worth. The same for those aspects of ourselves we might despise or see as loathsome; they contain value for our spiritual transformation in that they have something to teach us—if we will observe them without self-condemnation. Above all, our less-than-perfect selves keep us humble and united with all human beings who contain their own set of imperfections.

REFLECTION

Look at your hands. Study them for their shape, color, and general appearance. You most probably do not think your hands are "perfect" or look as good as you'd like them to look. Yet your life would be drastically altered without them. Can you also accept your less-than-perfect self with a similar recognition and appreciation? Write a letter of kindness to the part of yourself that you least like.

PRAYER

Source of Love, turn me around to look at myself, to see as you see, to love as you love, to accept as you accept, that I may approach myself with a heart of loving-kindness.

SCRIPTURE TO CARRY IN YOUR HEART TODAY

"'My grace is sufficient for you, for power is made perfect in weakness.' So, I will boast all the more gladly of my weaknesses, so that the power of Christ may dwell in me" (2 Cor 12:9).

WEEK 2, DAY 5

COMPASSION FATIGUE

The self is limited. It has only so much energy. If it is not renewed, then depletion will take place. Too often we don't avail ourselves of the type of activities that truly renew us. When this occurs we run a greater risk that we will unnecessarily lose perspective and burn out.

—Robert J. Wicks, *Riding the Dragon*[24]

No one can keep pouring out large amounts of compassion without eventually becoming emptied of mental, emotional, and physical energy—unless they are also nurturing and replenishing that love by attentive self-compassion. Without it, persons whose work or life situation requires them to tend to the suffering of others will find their motivation hindered by negativity and their ability to care trapped in what is commonly termed "compassion fatigue" or "secondary traumatic stress disorder."

Research shows that "nearly one out of five American adults serves as a caregiver to a loved one—an elderly parent or in-law in almost half of cases but in other instances a spouse, a child or other relative who has become sick or disabled. . . . Decades of research tally the toll: poorer health, financial sacrifice, depression and anxiety."[25]

Henri Nouwen learned a lot about this during his years of caring for adults with mental and emotional disabilities:

> Caregiving is a deeply ingrained human response to suffering. We want to ease pain, to restore calm and peace to those in need. But caregiving takes a toll. There is often a huge cost to the caregiver, and

sometimes the care we give springs not from a well of love and altruism but from a bitter sea of resentful duty and obligation. It is hard to listen to others when the pains and troubles of our own lives are clamoring for attention.

But if we listen to our needs and wants, that listening can free us to learn to become truly present to the inner deep and fragile beauty of those under our care. Then even the most mundane and repetitive caregiving tasks can become a means for us to grow. With patience, with time, we can develop relationships of respect, listening, presence, and truthfulness with those we care for.[26]

Numerous authors have described specific signs of compassion fatigue. Some of these include constant negativity, misdirected anger and blaming, calloused indifference, taking on a martyr attitude, arrogance and hostility, weariness that never leaves (regardless of sleep), physical ailments without a specific cause (such as backaches, stomach problems, headaches, anxiety, and nervous issues), and a growing lack of enthusiasm and kindness. We can be quite sure compassion fatigue is setting in when some aspect of our body, mind, or spirit continually rebels or resists vigorously in extending care to others.

I recognized symptoms of compassion fatigue during a conversation with nurses from a neonatal intensive care unit. They described an incident from a few weeks earlier when they were startled by how their head nurse mocked and made fun of a mother's uncontrolled outburst. This mother had been coming to visit her fragile child for more than five months—a visit of sixty miles twice a day, before and after her full day of work. Finally, the stress was too much, and she completely lost her composure. At the same time, the head nurse was overworked and unable to debrief about the constant sadness arising from infant deaths that took place in her unit. Consequently, she slipped into one of compassion fatigue's dreaded symptoms: cynicism. Both the director and the mother responded as they did because of the constant, unbearable weight of caregiving while neglecting compassion for self.

A different dimension of compassion fatigue appeared the day that LuAnn came to visit me. I opened the door and felt shocked to see that much of her hair had fallen out and how terribly thin she had become in a little more than a month. I prepared myself to hear that she had cancer. Instead, I learned that her physical condition resulted from an inability to ward off tensions from the endless demands of her church ministry. Her body was informing her of the perilous results if she did not stop and tend to her own needs.

Among the ways that we can help prevent compassion fatigue, the following remain central: lowering our expectations of how much we can do; being careful not to be consumed by others' sorrow and hurt; being less attached to the outcome or success of our work; setting boundaries around our time and presence; refusing to believe we are indispensable; and avoiding the desire to fix another person's problems or difficulties.

Learning to be compassionate toward ourselves is a lifelong process. We learn and forget, learn and forget. If we keep returning in prayer to the One who knows and loves us completely, we will continue in our efforts to care well for ourselves, and keep getting better at doing so.

REFLECTION

Make a list of the ways your energy becomes depleted. Make another list of the ways that you restore your energy. Which list is longer? What does that tell you about your self-care?

PRAYER

Divine Caregiver, you are rest for the weary, solace for the sorrowful, kindness for those who are worn out. Wrap your tender loving-kindness around me. Slow me down when I career closely to the cliff of compassion fatigue by too much concern for others and too little for myself.

SCRIPTURE TO CARRY IN YOUR HEART TODAY

"Come to me, all you that are weary and are carrying heavy burdens, and I will give you rest" (Mt 11:28).

WEEK 2, DAY 6

PRACTICING SELF-COMPASSION

*To transform the suffering in our stories into a
meaningful experience requires a courageous
heart and a keen spiritual alertness.*

—Gail Straub, *The Rhythm of Compassion*[27]

Volumes of recommendations for self-care fill magazine racks and bookstore shelves. The following story offers a superb example of approaching ourselves compassionately. In an article titled "Freed Speech," Caridade Drago describes the shame and humiliation he experienced due to stammering. He constantly feared rejection when he spoke. A turning point came when he was a novice in his religious community, and his spiritual director suggested that the stammering came from something other than a physical condition. The possibility of this truth stung

Caridade so severely that he made a decision to finally face his deep pain.

His spiritual guide counseled Caridade to meditate and be compassionate toward himself, and Caridade wisely and courageously followed that advice:

> I learned to sit erect and still and to be in the presence of God, who is the ocean of compassion. I watched every feeling that arose in my heart and every thought that passed through my mind. I owned them as mine and placed them before God. . . . At the beginning, the river of painful experiences began to rise and inundate me. I had to make a concerted effort to stand in the strong currents of feelings and thoughts like a tree. The river was nothing but my fears, anger and brokenness seeking attention and healing. In the presence of God and with his help, I learned to see those who had hurt me through the eyes of Jesus, the compassion of God made visible. I perceived my own self and others sailing in the same boat. Regular practice of remaining in the compassionate presence made me compassionate to my own self and others. It doubled my self-confidence and reduced my fears.[28]

Caridade Drago's experience touches my heart and assures me of the power of self-compassion to heal and transform. He chose to befriend his hurt and bravely gave himself in trust to the divine Healer. In doing so, Caridade's self-compassion led not only to feeling less isolated, but also to being more connected to others through his compassion.

When Kristin Neff details components of self-compassion, she includes "our common humanity." Neff observes that when we experience life as difficult or not going the way we wish, we often have a "pervasive sense of isolation . . . as if 'I' were the only person suffering or making mistakes. All humans suffer. . . . Therefore, self-compassion involves recognizing that suffering and personal inadequacy is part of . . . something we all go through rather than being something that happens to 'me' alone."[29]

When I remember *our common humanity*—that a form of my experience also happens to others—this reality comforts me. The first time I traveled alone overseas I eased my fear by thinking, *A lot of people around the world are traveling alone today, just as I am. I will be okay.* Sensing that oneness calmed my anxiety and gave me strength. Another time, when I was in the laborious process of moving after living in the same place for twenty years, I paused and said to myself, *At this very moment, countless other people are also leaving places they have grown fond of and find painful to leave.* Again, that thought eased my emotional state. The reluctance and grief lessened. My heavy heart felt lighter. I knew I could do what was required.

Another aspect of Caridade Drago's healing experience that catches my attention is his openness to his spiritual director's counsel. Had he not done so, his stuttering might still be afflicting him. Oftentimes, our struggle with key issues leaves us unable to resolve them without the aid of skilled psychological, spiritual, or physical assistance. It takes a certain humbleness to acknowledge that we require others in our process of self-compassion. We may feel embarrassed, or not wish to be "in debt" to anyone for our well-being.

A sense of low self-worth can also affect our hesitation to accept assistance. We may not believe that we are worthy of another's kindness or that we deserve to be the recipient of their time and attention. Another deterrent to receiving compassion from others may be an unintentional oblivion to our own needs, so intent are we in giving generously to others that we ignore our personal health of body, mind, and spirit.

Humility, vulnerability, openness, awareness—each of these affects our readiness to receive, especially when we are depleted of energy or emptied of self-worth. Whatever the situation, receptivity to others' compassionate care for us remains an essential part of tending to ourselves.

REFLECTION

Locate a large, empty bowl. Sit down and place the bowl in your lap. Look into the emptiness. Is there any part of your current situation that compares to this emptiness? Hold the empty bowl up. Open your heart with a readiness to receive what you need to in order to care for yourself. Set the bowl back down. Make a resolution to be ready to receive the gift offered to you by the Holy One.

PRAYER

Guardian of My Soul, thank you for the persons who have come into my life and assisted in my ability to be compassionate toward myself.

SCRIPTURE TO CARRY IN YOUR HEART TODAY

"Let me hear of your steadfast love in the morning,

for in you I put my trust.

Teach me the way I should go,

for to you I lift up my soul." (Ps 143:8)

WEEK 2, DAY 7

REVIEW AND REST

To know how to receive, that is also a most important gift,
which cultivates generosity in others and keeps strong the
cycle of life. If the heart knows not how to share . . . then
that heart is closed off from receiving and closes off the free
flow of others' giving. . . . Giving, receiving—one breath.

—Dhyani Ywahoo, *Voices of Our Ancestors*[30]

Choose any or all of the following as a way to review Week Two:

- What three aspects of "Welcoming Ourselves" were of greatest significance to you this past week?

- In what ways might this week's focus on self-compassion make a difference in how you live?

- Of the quotations used this week, which one stands out as containing the best insight for your self-compassion growth?

- Which day's reflection challenged you the most?

- Which one left you nodding your head yes?

- As you look back over the week, were there moments or situations that awakened your self-compassion?

- Go back to Day 4. Do the exercise of William Miller that is described there. Sit with your spit. Let it tell you about the parts of yourself that you do not like.

- Look back over Week Two. Notice the various ways you extended compassion to yourself. List these. Read over them, and after each one whisper, "Thank you."

WEEK THREE

The RIVER OF SUFFERING

INTRODUCTION

I saw the river over which every soul must pass
to reach the kingdom of heaven,
and the name of that river was suffering:
and I saw the boat which carries souls across the river,
and the name of that boat was love.

—St. John of the Cross, "River of Suffering"[1]

When I speak to a group, I can be quite sure that each person there knows about suffering from personal experience. Our society idolizes happiness and subtly insists that we hide our wounds. People smile and appear happy. Yet the burdens and wounded places of the human heart are not far from any one of us. Underneath those smiles all sorts of unresolved hurt manage to reside. We are all making our way across the river of suffering, and every soul benefits from being carried in the boat named *love*.

In *Entering the Healing Ground*, Francis Weller names principal areas related to suffering and the ensuing grief. The first relates to the impermanence of life. Nothing stays the same; consequently, our life eventually loses some of the people and things we value. The next loss consists of the places within us that have lived outside of our "kindness, compassion, warmth, or welcome." Another area of suffering results from the "collective sorrow" of the world of which we are a part. The fourth loss comes from our dreams and the intangible longings that "we expected and did not receive." The fifth one Weller mentions is that of "ancestral grief," the unhealed sorrow inherited from our ancestors who were unable to tend to their loss.[2] Weller adds yet another source of our loss in a later book, *The Wild Edge of Sorrow*: trauma or soul loss: "when the desire for life . . . becomes so blunted that death becomes appealing and depression a way of life."[3]

A cottonwood tree that stands tall and lean by Lake Michigan has taught me about responding to the unwanted losses that Weller describes. Each time I visit Racine, Wisconsin, I stand for quite a while looking at the tree that I call my sentinel of strength. A long swath of stripped-off bark along one side of the trunk bears evidence of its having been struck by lightning. I often ask the tree, "How have you endured? What is your secret?" Each time I hear one word: "Resiliency."

Each of us contains that gift. Human beings not only have the power to survive and bounce back after inevitable loss, but they also are able to shape *how* they enter into this recovery. We can do more than endure our sufferings. Depending on our responses, suffering provides untold opportunities for inner transformation. "Loss, ironically enough, is the catalyst of newness," writes Benedictine Joan Chittister. It is "a doorway to other parts of the soul, where what lies dormant in us comes alive because come alive it must."[4]

Langston Hughes's verse, "My soul has grown deep like rivers," conveys the power of suffering to transform us.[5] The energizing flow of rivers through land and rock often sculpts magnificent canyons and passageways. The river becomes a metaphor for suffering's power to transform the human spirit. It may take years, as does a river, to carve something new in our life, to form a passageway to another expression of the soul as yet unlived. At the same time, we dare not idealize suffering as the only way to personal growth. Joy also transforms. Ask anyone who has received unconditional love, been forever influenced by a moment of nature's beauty, or known the unexpected departure of a terminal illness.

Week Three focuses on the reality of suffering and our stance toward it. While the questions of why suffering happens and how God is involved elude satisfactory answers, we *do* have the assurance of this compassionate Presence being with us. One of the most tender descriptions comes from Henri Nouwen and his coauthors: "God's compassion is total, absolute, unconditional, without reservation. It is the compassion of the one who keeps going to the most forgotten corners of the world, and who cannot rest as long as there are still human beings with tears in their eyes."[6]

Christians recognize this characteristic of divinity by the manner in which Jesus entered into his suffering. In *God in Pain*, Barbara Brown Taylor explains it this way:

> We need a God who knows about pain. . . . It is not all that popular an idea, even among Christians. We prefer a God who prevents suffering, only that is not the God we have got. What the cross teaches us is that God's power is not the power to force human choices and end human pain. It is, instead, the power to pick up the shattered pieces and make something holy out of them—not from a distance but right close up.[7]

I invite you this week to "pick up the shattered pieces" of your experience of suffering and observe what you have learned. As you do so, reflect on how you continue to grow in becoming a compassionate presence because of how these sufferings have visited your life.

WEEK 3, DAY 1

RESPONDING TO SUFFERING

There is not always a solution to suffering
but there is always a possible response.
—Christina Feldman, *Compassion*[8]

In addressing the topic of compassion, the subject of suffering must be included. As we become aware of what shapes our attitude toward suffering, we gain insight into how to approach both our own and others' suffering in a way that encourages compassion. Rather than denying, ignoring, or resisting the unwanted hurts, we enter them with empathy. We also avoid projecting our views about inevitable suffering when we become aware of what shapes our thinking about it.

Christina Feldman emphasizes the necessity of being with our suffering: "Compassion will remain a closed door as long as you close your heart to an awareness and acceptance of pain. Opening to the sorrow that exists inwardly and outwardly is simultaneously opening to the boundless compassion that can emerge from your heart."[9] The life of South African president and antiapartheid activist Nelson Mandela exemplifies this kind of response. During the twenty-seven years he spent in prison, eighteen of them in brutal and oppressive Robben Island, he managed to stay free from developing animosity and a hardened heart. Historians attribute this to Mandela's deliberate effort to find unity with the other prisoners, along with a desire to be kind and forgiving to all, including the guards. Mandela's years of suffering in confinement honed and widened his compassion. He left prison with an astounding spirit of hope and openness.

Nelson Mandela decided how he would respond to his suffering. His response seems exceptional, but the lives of wounded persons everywhere attest to the possibility of being changed positively. Barbara Brown Taylor offers a central reason for why this is possible: "There is a difference between pain and suffering. . . . Pain originates in the body. . . . Pain happens in the flesh. . . . Suffering . . . happens in the mind. The mind decides what pain means and whether it is deserved. The mind notices who comes to visit and who does not. The mind remembers how good things used to be and are not likely to be again. The mind makes judgments, measures loss, takes blame, and assigns guilt."[10]

Some people remain broken and bereft by unbendable resentment, ongoing hostility, unresolved grief, distressing traumatic memories, and nonforgiveness. Inner disturbances can refuse to budge and remain unmanageable for a long time. Other factors also exist that might prevent healing and the growth of compassion: the severity of the experience, learned behavior from childhood, and a lack of inner resources and support to help cope with distress. Beliefs about the cause of suffering also determine whether the heart widens or narrows.

How we are with our own suffering will certainly affect how we respond to others who suffer, especially if we think they ought to respond in the way we do. For example, if I believe it is best to ignore or deny my pain, I will expect others to do the same. When my friend's bruised body and broken foot prevented her from traveling for a speaking engagement, the coordinator of the event chided her for the decision to cancel with the comment, "I flew to Norway with a cast on my leg. Surely you can come here."

The projection of religious beliefs onto others who suffer also affects compassion. When my cousin faced the last year of her life due to ovarian cancer, two Bible-toting women came to her bedside and assured her that if she "just had enough faith" she would not die. They thought they were being compassionate, but their religious beliefs robbed my cousin of a serene death. She clung absolutely to their assurance and died without the peaceful acceptance of turning toward death, or of saying good-bye to her two young daughters.

In his essay "The Suffering of Christ," theologian Michael Himes writes:

> Often it is thought, not least by theologians, that the theological task is to provide persuasive answers to religious questions. It is not. Theology's task is to clarify exactly how difficult, how puzzling, and how pressing the questions are. . . . Theology is at its most distorted when it convinces us that all the pieces of our experience fit together, that all the puzzles are solved, that all the answers have been given, in short, when it does away with suffering. Faith that assures us that following Jesus means taking up a cross of precisely the right weight and walking a perfectly straight road is false faith. . . . True faith demands that we see and feel how immensely deep and how darkly mysterious the experience of being a human being is. . . . Religious faith does not take away suffering or make it easier.[11]

Can religious faith make a difference in how we suffer? The response of Jesus to his suffering offers reassurance. He entered into his suffering on the Cross after struggling to avoid it. Jesus leaned on the Holy One's strength and entrusted his entire being into this great Love as he breathed his last (see Lk 23:46). I have often gained strength to enter my own suffering by knowing I was not alone, that this compassionate Presence understood my suffering and accompanied my every step toward healing.

While we naturally resist suffering, at some point we turn toward it if we are to receive the inherent growth that awaits us. In *Eternal Echoes*, John O'Donohue writes:

> The strange thing is: the more you resist [suffering], the longer it stays. . . . When you stop resisting suffering, something else begins to happen. There is in suffering some hidden shadowed light. Destiny has a perspective on us and our pathway that we can never fully glimpse; it alone knows why suffering comes. Suffering has its own reasoning. It wants to teach us something. When you stop resisting its dark work, you are open to learning what it wants to show you. . . . Suffering is the sister of your future possibility.[12]

Join hands with suffering, and let her lead you toward compassion.

REFLECTION

What do you believe about suffering? How have your difficulties been a catalyst for the way you approach others in their sufferings?

PRAYER

Bearer of the Cross, your struggle with the mystery of suffering assures me that I will find strength to carry my own cross, if I lean on the Eternal Love as you did. Lead me through the valley of darkness with your abiding compassion.

SCRIPTURE TO CARRY IN YOUR HEART TODAY

"Trust in [God] at all times, O people;

pour out your heart before [God];

God is a refuge for us." (Ps 62:8)

WEEK 3, DAY 2

THE GIFT OF EMPATHY

In the first step toward a compassionate heart,
we must develop our empathy or closeness to others.

—Dalai Lama, *An Open Heart*[13]

In *The Art of Empathy*, Karla McLaren defines this quality as "a social and emotional skill that helps us feel and understand the emotions, circumstances, intentions, thoughts, and needs of others, such that we can offer sensitive, perceptive, and appropriate communication and support."[14] That definition sounds too clinical. I much prefer that of Franciscan author Ilia Delio: "Compassion is the ability to 'get inside the skin of another' in order to respond with loving concern and care. It is a deep connectedness to another; one breathes in the pain of the other and breathes out compassion. The compassionate person identifies with the suffering of others in such a way that she or he makes a space within the heart to allow the suffering of another to enter, not to heal them or remove their pain but to be with them in solidarity."[15]

Empathy enables us to be compassionately present to another's wounds. Without empathy, compassion lacks heart and easily becomes mere burden. Empathy establishes a relationship with those who suffer and keeps us from standing apart with a pitying posture toward them.

The gospels depict Jesus as being moved with compassion. When he comes in contact with the people's suffering, he senses deeply what it must be like for them to be hungry, harassed, dejected, blind, paralyzed, grieving, or continually ill. An example is when Jesus' friend Lazarus, the brother of Martha and Mary, had died: "When Jesus saw [Mary] weeping, and the Jews who came with her also weeping, he was greatly disturbed in spirit and deeply moved" (Jn 11:33). The Greek verb for "to be moved" is *splangchnizomai*, meaning a deep, intense response. The word *splangchna* actually refers to the entrails of the body. Thus, the translation might read that Jesus had "a strong, gut response" when he met suffering in another. It was *so* like him to be "lost with the lost, hungry with the hungry, and sick with the sick," as Henri Nouwen writes.[16]

Although humans are born with the capacity for empathy, this natural trait can be hidden or rejected. In an interview, oncology physician Raymond Barfield was asked, "Do you think you can teach medical students empathy?" Barfield responded, "I think humans are inclined to feel empathy, but empathy can be crushed. Something seems to happen in medical school and residency that dulls our sense of empathy. It's dulled by discussing illness and interventions in ways that don't acknowledge patients and physicians as people. It's dulled by the volume of suffering encountered in the course of training. It's dulled by mere fatigue. . . . The answer is yes. Physicians can remember what it is to be human."[17]

Not just physicians lose their empathy. Our competitive, politically abrasive, self-oriented culture tends to shove empathy aside as well. All of us need to remember what it is to be human. We move from being an outsider to an insider if we listen with an open mind and heart to what another person is experiencing.

Oftentimes our own suffering serves to elicit a sense of empathy. In his memoir of St. Teresa of Calcutta, Brian Kolodiejchuk, M.C., writes with admiration of her astounding empathy for society's most vulnerable. He points out that Mother Teresa's personal suffering from her spiritual aridity and darkness instilled in her an immense compassion: "This interior and excruciating pain of feeling unwanted, unloved, unclaimed by God whom she loved with her whole heart, enabled her to grasp what the homeless felt in their daily life. She completely identified with their misery, loneliness, and rejection. And the poor felt this deep compassion of hers, merciful and nonjudgmental; they felt welcomed, loved, and understood."[18]

Such examples are more common than you might think. It was Jim Dodge's physical suffering that occasioned his ever-growing empathy. After he came back from serving in the Vietnam War, Jim developed Hodgkin's disease as a result of being exposed to Agent Orange. He spent the rest of his life as a chronically ill man with a walking disability from cancer treatments. Jim's experiences with suffering led him to use his talents as a certified public accountant to cofound an organization to help marginalized people with their income taxes. Jim did not stop there. After graduating with a master's in divinity degree, he went on to organize City House, an amazing nonprofit in Minneapolis where spiritual directors tend to the spiritual needs of disenfranchised and homeless persons.

There are several accounts of how the seed of empathy was sown in abolitionist Levi Coffin's young heart. His family owned slaves. One version describes how Levi was only eight or nine when the family of one of the male slaves was sold to work elsewhere, except for the father of that family, who remained behind. Levi's father couldn't understand why the slave was visibly filled with grief. He asked the slave what was wrong. When Levi heard the slave describe his sorrow at losing his family, it disturbed Levi greatly. That experience birthed Levi's desire to bring slavery to an end because he sensed the pain in that father's heart.[19]

Empathy also develops in us as a result of reading memoirs and other personal accounts of suffering. For example, after reading prisoners' descriptions of what it is like for them to be incarcerated, a woman wrote to a magazine editor: "I don't know anyone in prison, but *The Sun* has made me feel like I do. After reading prisoner's contributions to your magazine, I find I have more empathy for them."[20]

Too much empathy can be as detrimental as too little. Excessively empathic people tend to overstep boundaries, project personal thoughts and feelings onto the person who suffers, and divert attention away from the sufferer and onto themselves. Imbalanced empathy actually creates more pain, rather than alleviating it. Having empathy does not require that we always "feel" the hurt of someone else. Empathy is more than an emotional response. It requires that we comprehend or sense someone's pain, so much so that we can be with him or her in a supportive manner. When we have empathy, we truly care about the person who suffers.

REFLECTION

Recall a time when someone was able to understand what you were going through. How did that person's empathy affect you?

PRAYER

Shepherd of Souls, incline my heart toward the direction of those who suffer. Let me lean in to catch the pungent scent of their pain, close enough to assure them of my understanding heart.

SCRIPTURE TO CARRY IN YOUR HEART TODAY

"Jesus called his disciples and said to them, 'I have compassion for the crowd, because they have been with me now for three days and have nothing to eat. If I send them away hungry to their homes, they will faint on the way—and some of them have come from a great distance'" (Mk 8:2–3).

WEEK 3, DAY 3

THE PATTERN OF TRANSFORMATION

Meaning does not change the particulars of our lives;
it changes our experience of those particulars.

—Rachel Naomi Remen, MD,
Kitchen Table Wisdom[21]

Our suffering may never make sense, but if we can find a reason or a meaning to go on with life, our resiliency will outlive the suffering. I discovered this for myself when I searched for solace and resolution after my twenty-five-year-old brother drowned. Fifteen years after that tragedy, with sorrow still bearing down on me, I went on a thirty-day retreat. This graced period of prayer opened the doorway to peace. During the retreat, I read and reflected on the journey of Jesus. There I encountered his life, death, and resurrection. I gradually recognized how these three aspects of transformation are a part of change and growth in many dimensions of existence.

The life of Jesus assured me that suffering and death are not the end of the story. Each year when Holy Week approaches, Christians prepare to relive the final days of Jesus' earthly life.

The liturgical services abound with this pattern of life-death-re-birth, reminding those present of the prerequisite for transformation. Holy Week brings to the forefront of reality what Jesus expressed in his teaching: "Unless a grain of wheat falls into the earth and dies, it remains just a single grain; but if it dies, it bears much fruit" (Jn 12:24).

Capuchin priest Edward Foley likens the process of Jesus' final days to our own: "The death and resurrection of the Lord is not a past event we reenact through the tableaus of Holy Week. Rather, it is a dynamic mystery that plays out in the holy chaos of our lives. We prepare for the wedding and lose the parent; nurture the child when abandoned by the spouse; get the job and lose the friend. Life is Holy Week, in all of its unpredictability."[22]

The transitional cycle of life-death-rebirth resides in our psyches from the moment of leaving the comfort of our mother's womb until the moment of our death. This pattern of *letting go of what is in order to welcome what can be* has established itself in numerous dimensions of life—such as the seasonal cycles of Earth: autumn lets go of summer's fullness and enters into winter's fallowness, which then gives way to spring's vibrant new life. We see this transition in the shedding of a snake's skin and the shell of a mollusk to allow their bodies to expand; in husks of seeds falling away before green shoots move upward; in caterpillars dying inside the chrysalis so butterflies can take form; in birds molting old feathers to make room for the new. All of these essential changes indicate the necessity and value that the pattern of life-death-rebirth indicates.

Finding meaning in this process may not "change the particulars of our lives," as Rachel Naomi Remen indicates, but it can proffer enough strength and resilience to stay in the fray until new life develops. Five years after the horrific shooting and death of children and teachers at the school in Newtown, Massachusetts, parents of the children were interviewed. One mother remarked that the most meaningful sermon she ever heard came during the funeral for her child when the minister suggested that everyone goes through the four seasonal cycles. The parents had been thrust into a harsh winter. At this point, the commentator asked, "Is there a springtime for you?" The mother responded, "I cannot imagine a springtime now. It is a long, hard winter." Being able to name her pain as a wintertime strengthened this mother in her grief, even though the possibility of something beyond it seemed impossible at the present time.

When suffering arrives with the cold breath of winter, we dwell in a tomb-like dormancy between death and resurrection. We rarely sense the stirrings of new life during this season. We have to trust that the gray, insecure period of uncertainty holds a promise of giving rise to an unforeseen gift. Things are not always what they seem. Something concealed is happening. We often fight this incubating period much as the cells of a dying caterpillar in a chrysalis fight off the birthing cells of the monarch butterfly. Their dying cells continue to resist until the monarch's cells strengthen enough to take on a life of their own.

When the talented German composer Ludwig van Beethoven learned of his impending deafness, he became frightened and depressed. He left Vienna, went to a cottage to be by himself, and contemplated suicide. He wrote a farewell letter to his brother that was only discovered after Beethoven's death twenty-five years later. No one knows how he transitioned from an intention of death to that of embracing life, but Beethoven managed to move beyond that despondency. He returned to Vienna with an acceptance of deafness and a renewed passion to create. The gift of Beethoven's cottage dormancy came alive in the nearly one hundred pieces of his greatest music after his return.[23]

One of our Boundless Compassion retreatants, Rita, described the process she went through after her son died of leukemia: "Daniel was given five years of life after his initial treatment. When he was again taken ill, my life stopped. I left my job to be with him. When Daniel died twenty years ago, I was unable to function. Sitting at home one day, I realized how angry he would be with me; Daniel loved life and filled every moment with reaching out to others. I returned to teaching, but I could not continue as before. I became certified as an ESL [English as a Second Language] teacher, got a job, and loved it. After retiring, another woman and I cofounded Literacy Volunteers on the Green—which has trained hundreds of tutors and served about a thousand students."[24]

Little did Rita know during her winter time, when she grieved the death of her son, that she would gain a new and satisfying way of teaching, one that contributed to many in the maintenance and improvement of their quality of life. This is the mystery of suffering and the gift it can birth in us—if we allow divine grace and the healing process enough time to gestate something fresh for our life.

REFLECTION

"In the mystery of suffering there are very few answers. But by breathing into the mystery, we will find our capacity for compassion. It will come in living the questions raised by our suffering not into answers but into acts of love" (Fr. Joseph Nassal, *The Conspiracy of Compassion*).[25]

What gives meaning to your life in regard to suffering?

PRAYER

Holy One, grant that I may have enough faith and patience to wait for the slow unfolding of new life that comes after the transition of leaving behind and letting go. Restore my hope when it fizzles out.

SCRIPTURE TO CARRY IN YOUR HEART TODAY

"Unless a grain of wheat falls into the earth and dies, it remains just a single grain; but if it dies, it bears much fruit" (Jn 12:24).

WEEK 3, DAY 4

BROKEN OPEN

*As your heart breaks open, there will be
room for the world to heal.*

—Joanna Macy, *World as Lover, World as Self* [26]

On the fifteenth anniversary of the terrorist attack on the World Trade Center, I listened to an interview on National Public Radio with a CEO who lost more than six hundred of his employees that day, including his own brother. The CEO's life was spared because he was taking his son to kindergarten that morning when the planes struck the towers. In spite of the enormous loss of staff, the company survived. Each year on the anniversary of September 11, this CEO asks his employees to give that day's pay to charity. They have given $12 million in those fifteen years, evidence that when suffering creates an obstacle that breaks a heart, it creates an opening for compassion to pour forth.

Parker Palmer ponders this reality in *Healing the Heart of Democracy*:

> We will never fully understand why people respond
> so differently to experiences of heartbreak: there is
> an eternal mystery about how the shattered soul be-
> comes whole again. But people whose hearts break

open, not apart, are usually those who have embraced life's "little deaths" over time, those small losses, failures, and betrayals that can serve as practice runs for the larger deaths yet to come. Some people do this intentionally as a function of their spiritual practice or reflective philosophy of life. Others do it because life takes them to places where it is either "do or die."[27]

Bryan Stevenson, Alabama trial lawyer for death-row inmates, relates a tender story of a grandmother whose broken heart transformed into a vessel of compassion. When Stevenson first encountered this older black woman in a courthouse hallway where he was working on the release of a prisoner, she gave him a kind smile and a warm hug. He was touched by that gesture and asked about her presence there. She told the lawyer, "I just come here to help people. This place is full of pain, so people need plenty of help around here." As they continued the conversation, he learned about her sixteen-year-old grandson's murder years earlier. She loved the boy and "grieved and grieved and grieved." She also cried for the boys who were convicted of killing her grandson. At their sentencing, a stranger in the courtroom came over, gave her an immense hug, and sat with her for more than two hours. This experience generated the grieving grandmother's compassion. A year later she began coming regularly to the courthouse to comfort those who had someone on trial and also those suffering from the crime that was committed. She concluded her story by saying: "I decided that I was supposed to be here to catch some of the stones people cast at each other."[28]

In her poem "Kindness," Naomi Shihab Nye describes how suffering like the grandmother's acts as a stimulus for compassion. The first two lines declare that we "must lose things" before we know "what kindness really is." Nye follows this wise observation by insisting that we must be willing to engage with sorrow, bring it into our life as fully as possible—wake up with it, speak to it—until it is fully a part of us. Only then will kindness permeate our whole being, go with us "like a shadow or a friend," and unite us with the sorrows of the world.[29]

St. John of the Cross, a Carmelite monk of the sixteenth century, also experienced an opening of his heart because of significant obstacles. When there were conflicts within his community, these disagreements eventually led to the members imprisoning John in a small, damp cell. John lived there in almost total darkness, facing hunger and beatings, along with a profound experience of spiritual angst. During his nine months in that confinement, some of John's most beautiful love poems to God emerged from the depths of his soul. When John finally escaped his imprisonment, he left with a spirit on fire with love.

Rather than deadening his monk's heart, John's suffering broke open a passion for the Holy One that could not be extinguished. His love and compassion for others who suffered also became heightened. John became known as "the patron of the afflicted" because of how compassionately he assisted others who knew the travails of life, whether materially or spiritually.[30]

Meditation teacher Jack Kornfield shares a valuable teaching about the gift of being broken open—a story from the Jewish mystical tradition:

> A great rabbi taught his disciples to memorize and contemplate the teachings and to place the prayers and holy words on their hearts. One day a student asked the rabbi why he always used the phrase "on your heart" and not "in your heart." The master replied, "Only time and grace can put the essence of these stories in your heart. Here we recite and learn

them and put them on our hearts hoping that some
day when our hearts break they will fall in."[31]

No one wants a broken heart. But when that happens, grace
finds an opening to flow into the stream of suffering.

REFLECTION

"Suffering can create an opening, the space, in the psyche's
structure that allows self-transcendence, that allows the release
of our own Essential splendor" (Kathleen Dowling Singh, *The
Grace in Dying*).[32]

How have your sufferings changed you? How have they
been catalysts for compassion?

PRAYER

Peace before me. Peace behind me. Peace under my feet. Peace
above me. Peace within me. Let all around me be peace. (Adapted from the Prayer of St. Patrick)

SCRIPTURE TO CARRY IN YOUR HEART TODAY

"God's love has been poured into our hearts through the Holy
Spirit that has been given to us" (Rom 5:5).

WEEK 3, DAY 5

COMPASSIONATE PRESENCE

*The face of the Divine in you recognizes the face of the
Divine in the other person. When you stand before one
another in this way, you are on holy ground.*

—James Miller and Susan Cutshall,
The Art of Being a Healing Presence[33]

Some experts refer to compassion as "the quivering of the heart."
I hesitate to use this definition because the heart does not always "quiver" in response to suffering. We do not always *feel*
like being compassionate. Sometimes it takes sheer willpower to
be there for someone with an illness or a difficulty that requires
our time and attentive presence. Caregivers understand this. No
matter how much they appreciate the person they are tending,
there are times when the heart feels sluggish with endless details
and must rely on the resolve of a loving commitment.

Compassion acknowledges the mutuality of a kindred presence in one another. Joyce Hutchison, oncology nurse and hos-
pice director, taught me this. People in her care, along with their
families and friends, were so profoundly touched by her compassionate presence that they rarely forgot it. The secret of Joyce's
presence came from a firm belief that each person in her care was
"another Christ." She saw the face of divinity in them. This inner
seeing transformed her ministry from "duty" to one of an endear-
ing, compassionate presence.

Scientific findings also support a mutuality between individuals. By placing two living heart cells (each with its own heartbeat) in separate petri dishes, researchers discovered that the
two heart cells eventually developed the same heartbeat. This

phenomenon, known as "entrainment," consists of two separate entities gradually growing in sync with one another, with the stronger of the two energies having the greatest influence. This mutual relationship results from entering each other's electromagnetic field. Scientists tell us that the human heart produces "two and a half watts of electrical energy with each heartbeat— enough to light a small electric light bulb. This energy forms an electromagnetic field that radiates out some twelve to fifteen feet beyond our body itself."[34] We know intuitively when we are in sync or out of sync with another person because we sense the energy of the other person's "field." If we are to be a compassionate presence, we will strive to have an electromagnetic field with a lot of loving-kindness emanating from us.

While compassion relies on an intertwining relationship with another, it is not about codependency, nor about becoming excessively responsible, nor about assuming another's pain. The process of compassion involves a delicate balance; we do what we can to help alleviate suffering but avoid being "fixers"—not hovering around, butting in, or acting like some sort of savior, like thinking, *without me, they won't get well, can't change, or will be unable to die peacefully.* It may seem to be a compassionate response when we allow ourselves to take on another's sorrow or troubles, but, as Rabbi Rami Shapiro points out, this is detrimental, not helpful:

> You may think of compassion as sharing another's pain. But of what value is that to you or to the other? If I come to you in pain and you end up with the same pain, all we have done is add to the world's suffering. We have done nothing to alleviate it. I want you to understand my pain, to respond to it deeply, but not to take it on yourself. I want you to help me see what you see and what I cannot see. I want you to engage

my pain as if I were an actor in a drama you were watching. Mirror my experience, but don't embrace it as your own.[35]

"Not mine to manage, not mine to fix." This appropriate and healthy response of not taking suffering on to oneself came from a pastor in an attempt to avoid absorbing issues of her congregation. It kept her from taking responsibility for what was not hers to tend. This internal message does not mean we step away and ignore suffering or stop caring. Rather, if I take on your anger at injustice, then we've added to the anger and done nothing about injustice; if I absorb your grief, there's simply more sorrow—it has not gone away; if I join in your complaints about your divorce, there's more bitterness. Instead, I listen as fully as I can, being present in such a way that you know I understand your pain and will be supportive for as long as it takes for your hurt to lessen. In this way, I join with your suffering and provide a compassionate presence.

Caring people who become in sync with us, even briefly, leave a lasting mark of kindness on our memory, whether we realize it or not. For example, a young woman whose father died met with a friend a few months after his passing. This friend explained her absence at the funeral services by saying, "I never go to them. I don't know what to say." To this the young woman who grieved her father replied, "I was in a daze the night of the wake. I do not remember anything anyone said—but I remember every person who spoke to me."

During a Boundless Compassion workshop, I overheard two women speaking about their surprise at seeing one another there. Liz was overjoyed to see Kate and thanked her immediately for the compassionate note she had sent when Liz's five-day-old child died. Kate was amazed that after twenty years Liz still remembered that message. Kate did not remember the child dying or the note she sent, but Liz never forgot the understanding and kindness that came with Kate's message.

In these and other accounts, I sense a deep resonance of compassionate presence much like that expressed by theologian Elizabeth Johnson: "In effect, the voice of God says to the caregiver: Come, I will send you to bring my presence, warmth, and help to those suffering persons in and through your own human heart and expert care."[36]

We are all capable of doing this very thing. We can sync our hearts with the hearts of those who carry heavy burdens and hurts.

REFLECTION

Think of a person in your life who is a compassionate person. This might be a relative, friend, or colleague, or a historical, biblical, religious, or literary figure. What is it about this person that draws you to think of him or her as a person of compassion?

PRAYER

Attune your heart to someone you know who is hurting. Visualize the tender warmth, deep peace, and healing love of divine compassion moving from head to foot through him or her.

SCRIPTURE TO CARRY IN YOUR HEART TODAY

"Blessed be . . . the God of all consolation, who consoles us in all our affliction, so that we may be able to console those who are in any affliction with the consolation with which we ourselves are consoled by God" (2 Cor 1:3–4).

WEEK 3, DAY 6

THE SHADOW SIDE OF COMPASSION

Look deeply inside yourself and ask,
What motivates me to serve?

—Gail Straub, *The Rhythm of Compassion*[37]

The first summer that I volunteered in one of the poorest areas in Appalachia, I discovered rather quickly how mixed my motivations were for being there. I felt excited about the opportunity to serve. I also thought I'd be doing something for "those people." I wanted my efforts to be fruitful and hoped to return home with a sense of pride in my achievements. I had not considered the possibility of the residents having something to teach me, that those I came to serve had valuable wisdom from their life experiences. Fortunately, when I arrived, the gentle pastor of the church sat down with me and said in a kindly but firm voice, "There is one thing I ask of you if you are going to work here: accept with an unconditional acceptance." In that brief request, the shadow side of my intentions exposed itself: I had set myself up as better than them, as a sort of mini-savior or do-gooder who would help "those poor people" to change their lives.

Whenever we extend any form of compassion, whether it be *mercy* in regard to forgiveness, *sympathy* for those who mourn, *justice* wherever it is lacking, *charity* to aid physically and materially, or *kindness* by our presence and skilled actions, our reasons for doing so usually carry mixed motivations. Some of these are healthy and genuine, while others derive their intentions from egotistic expectations and cloudy agendas, thus creating a shadow or hidden side of compassion.

Gail Straub explores a number of these shadow elements in *The Rhythm of Compassion*, including "shame, guilt, should, and spiritual arrogance; a need for self-esteem, approval, status, and power; a martyr complex that says, 'I can never do enough; if I stop serving, the world will fall apart.'" She adds other false motivations, as well: "condescension, voices of the ego: 'Look how great I am. Look how politically correct I am. I am better and especially more spiritually evolved than you are. Wait until so and so hears what I am doing.'"[38]

The shadow of compassion also involves "wanting to fix a person or an issue, to be in control or be the expert, becoming a service workaholic, or giving service based on rage and self-righteousness." Straub also mentions the kind of shadow I brought with me to Kentucky: "the illusion that we are better than those we serve." She warns that we might be shocked at how we feel when we recognize one or more of these shadows. Straub reminds us that if we are going to "unmask these shadow elements," we need to "look at them openly and compassionately, remembering that we all get to observe the unhealthy parts of our ego when we serve others."[39]

Straub thoughtfully asks the reader to remember that our shadow is "mixed in with our genuine desire to care."[40] While we want to be aware of any aspects of shadow that might thwart our effort to be compassionate, we also want to have a healthy, positive stance about our desire to be there with others.

I have had plenty of opportunities to "unmask my shadow." These include making the assumption that I know what someone else needs, instead of asking what he or she might want. This happened the day I joined a friend to bring lunch to a woman with terminal cancer. When we arrived, we noticed a considerable change in her physical condition: she now required the assistance of a walker. I immediately proceeded to bring a chair over for her to sit on so I could push her to the table, a few feet away. She quickly put out her hand in protest and said, "No! I need to do this myself." Then she ever so slowly stood up, took her walker, and inched her way to the table. In that moment I realized how my shadow almost kept her from still being able to have some control over her life.

A retired book publisher working as a volunteer in a food pantry explained how the shadow of self-righteous judgment became evident with a neighborhood woman who came regularly to receive food. The pantry allowed only so much food per person. This particular woman always tried to get around the regulation and receive more than her allotment. Gradually he became aware of his harsh thoughts: *She's so pushy. Who does she think she is? She ought to be grateful to get this food instead of trying to manipulate her way toward more.* This awareness humbled him and helped him to extend a warmer welcome.

Gail Straub notes another value in exposing the shadow side of our compassion: "The extraordinary thing is that service of any kind reveals the parts of you that still need healing. The shadows from your personal life follow you into the world, along with your skills for transforming them. . . . As you care for others, you will find your personal healing is accelerated in ways you never imagined."[41]

"Why am I doing this?" The clearer we are about our motivation for offering compassion, the less likely we are to pass on the unhealthy aspects of our intentions that accompany our desire to serve. The more honest we are regarding our motivations, the kinder we will be in extending compassion to others.

REFLECTION

Choose a current situation in which you care for another in some way (such as in your professional work, in your family, in a personal relationship, through church or social service, in a volunteer ministry, etc.). Reflect on your motivations for doing what you do.

PRAYER

May all I am and all I do come from the source of your love, Compassionate One.

SCRIPTURE TO CARRY IN YOUR HEART TODAY

"Let love be genuine" (Rom 12:9).

WEEK 3, DAY 7

REVIEW AND REST

Bearing the unbearable is the deepest root of compassion in the world. When you bear what you think you cannot bear, who you think you are dies. You become compassion. You don't have compassion—you are compassion. True compassion goes beyond empathy to being with the experience of another. You become an instrument of compassion.

—Ram Dass, *Polishing the Mirror*[42]

Choose any or all of the following as a way to review Week Three:

- What three aspects of "The River of Suffering" were of greatest significance to you this past week?

- Of the suffering you have experienced in your life and others, what have you found to be the most difficult in extending your compassion?

- If you were to write on a tombstone an epitaph that describes your experience of this week's topic, what would that one-liner be?

- Which day's reflection challenged you the most?

- Which one left you nodding your head yes?

- As you look back over the week, did some experience or insight help to clarify how suffering might have meaning in your life?

- Draw your "river of suffering."

  - ♦ On the river, write the perceived obstacles from the past that have caused suffering and distress in your life. Take a look at what you have placed on the river. Ask yourself: "What was my experience of these obstacles? How did they hinder the flow of my life?"

  - ♦ Choose one of these obstacles. Reflect on what, in particular, was hurtful or stressful about this hindrance. Write these aspects next to the hindrance. Ask yourself: "When did I become free from this obstacle? How did that change for me? Did some inner growth eventually take place because of this? If so, how?"

  - ♦ Draw a boat on the river. Inside of it write or draw symbols for the wisdom, growth, or newness that came to you because of your experience of this obstacle.

FROM HOSTILITY TO HOSPITALITY

INTRODUCTION

It is time to be prophetic about the Christ we know is
present in the folks who are pushed aside, dismissed,
left out, undetermined, unfed, unhoused,
or simply unseen and unheard.

—Robert Lentz and Edwina Gateley,
Christ in the Margins[1]

In *Across That Bridge*, Congressman John Lewis of Georgia recounts his first experience of marginalization. As a small boy he relished life in a rural area where he knew only the joy of acceptance. At six years old, that changed for John when he accompanied his father into town to sell some farm crops and buy supplies. That trip awakened Lewis to how the larger world viewed him. He watched the demeaning way young white men treated his father by calling him "boy" as they weighed the grain. His eyes met surprising signs that read: "white women," "colored women," "white men," "colored men." Suddenly he felt himself not in the center of life but shoved far out to its edge. Lewis knew for the first time the feeling of being seen as "inferior, a reject, a substandard creation."[2]

What is it like to stand on the margins of life, to be discounted as an insignificant outsider or a social miscreant? Have you been in a situation where you felt out of place, shunned for a lack of understanding and acceptance, ignored, or unable to have your ideas and suggestions heard? Have you known the privation of basic human rights, such as food, clothing, shelter, education, safety, literacy, freedom of speech, and freedom of religion? If so, you can comprehend what it means to be marginalized. These are people and groups whom society considers "less than" because they do not meet certain cultural standards and social expectations. Marginalized persons know what rejection is like, how it feels not to have a voice or an advocate, to experience hate and violent language used against them. Their pain of not belonging lives as a constant reminder of how far they are from the inner circle of society where people of privilege reside.

Jesus welcomed marginalized people. His heart had room for them all. After his sojourn in the wilderness, when he came forth to publicly live the way of compassion, he began teaching in the synagogues. On one of these occasions early in his ministry, Jesus unrolled a scroll with verses from Isaiah, using that prophet's words to announce his service to those who were disenfranchised: "The Spirit of the Lord is upon me, because he has anointed me to bring good news to the poor . . . to proclaim release to the captives and recovery of sight to the blind, to let the oppressed go free" (Lk 4:18).

The Second Vatican Council in its opening "Message to Humanity" urged the followers of Jesus to take to heart his concern for the afflicted:

> Coming together in unity from every nation under the sun, we carry in our hearts the hardships, the bodily and mental distress, the sorrows, longings, and hopes of all the peoples entrusted to us. We urgently turn our thoughts to all the anxieties by which [humankind] is afflicted. Hence, let our concern swiftly focus first of all on those who are especially lowly, poor, and weak. . . . We want to fix a steady gaze on those who still lack the opportune help to achieve a way of life worthy of human beings.[3]

This week I invite you to "fix a steady gaze" by stepping into the world of people who are marginalized. Each day encourages a view of that situation from another perspective, to understand the causes of this disparity among humankind, and to become more aware of what can be done to change those conditions. Henri Nouwen describes the challenge of accompanying people on the outer rim of society:

> In our world full of strangers, estranged from their own past, culture and country, from their neighbors, friends and family, from their deepest self and their God, we witness a painful search for a hospitable place where life can be lived without fear and where community can be found. Although many, we might even say most, strangers in this world become easily the victim of a fearful hostility, it is possible for men and women and obligatory for Christians to offer an open and hospitable space where strangers can cast off their strangeness and become our fellow human beings. The movement from hostility to hospitality is hard and full of difficulties.[4]

Each of us has within a vast heart with room enough to welcome those who have been left out and forgotten. Each of us has love enough to embrace with compassion the most vulnerable and dispossessed of our society. Each of us has enough material resources to ease the life of those who lack our abundance.

WEEK 4, DAY 1

THE HAVES AND THE HAVE-NOTS

*The richest eight people in the world own more
wealth between them than the poorest 50 percent of
humanity—3.6 billion people.*

—Jim Wallis, "Robin Hood in Reverse"[5]

What does it take for a privileged person to turn toward compassionate action? Statistics provide information about the immense economic disparity on the planet, but that is not enough. Guilt also rarely achieves compassionate action in this regard. Neither will constant haranguing. One of the most effective ways of shaking loose indifference and ignorance about the wide chasm between wealth and poverty comes from viewing it up close and personal.

Several years ago, I walked through London's Heathrow airport in early December. The terminal sparkled with Christmas glitter and glitz. I paused at one of the elegant stores to admire a lovely silk scarf, priced at £233 ($365). A bit stunned at the fact that someone would pay that amount for a scarf, I proceeded to find the departure gate. There, I sat down to continue reading Katherine Boo's *Beyond the Beautiful Forevers*, a potent book filled with true accounts of people living in Annawadi—one of the worst slums in Mumbai, India. Katherine Boo chose to live among the poorest of the poor for several years, listening to their stories and observing how they managed to get through each day. She came to know the waste pickers—young children who sort through stinking garbage to find items to sell for recycling. Few of these children receive a formal education. The tiny sheds the families live in are next to a lake filled with sewage. Rats bite the children as they sleep. It is a contemptible life but one the slum dwellers accept as their fate.

As I sat reading, I paused to consider my own privileged existence, recognizing that even something as simple as being able to read a book set me apart from the Annawadi people. I thought again about that expensive scarf and felt a great sadness at the disparity between someone buying a £233 scarf and a child pleased to make a few rupees for a hard day's work in a dangerous, rotting garbage dump. How is it that our world divides so unevenly between those who have and those who have not? How is it that many of the *haves* remain disinterested and make little effort to change this sinful disproportion?

Constricted self-interest keeps the "haves" from recognizing and doing something to lessen the situation of the "have nots." Removing this obstacle of self-orientation takes great determination to not succumb to our culture's addiction to consumerism, a culture that entices us to buy more, have more, be more. When our central focus is on what *we* want and what *we* think we need to have, the less we give our attention and concern to those who have little or nothing at all.

Disregarding those who suffer from economic destitution and social exclusion also stems from the habit of objectifying people on the margins, those who do not fit in with expected social customs and privileged behavior. Descriptive words such as *weird, crazy, bum, illegals, hillbillies, homeless, criminal, lazy, hicks* widen the divide and strengthen the superior attitude of those who *have*. Every time we label someone negatively, we push them out of our circle. We narrow the option of connection and communication and widen the distance between their life and ours.

Dr. Hosffman Ospino, assistant professor at Boston College, concurs:

There are words that people of privilege use in not-so-gracious ways to identify others: illegal, minority, alien, worthless, enemy. They say more about what's in the heart of the one who speaks them than they say about the individuals or groups so identified. These words embody one's failure to recognize the fullness of humanity of the other. They hinder the flourishing of relationships. They prevent us from contemplating the *imago Dei*, the image of God, in our midst.[6]

The greater the gap we put between ourselves and others, the less likely we will empathize with their situation and act on their behalf.

On my way to the airport from a retreat center in New England, a taxi driver told me proudly of his Catholic school education from an early age through college. He then expounded on his view of people living in poverty, quipping that they all "slept until noon and didn't do a damn thing." He added, "They can live here, but I don't want any of *my* money going to *them*." His remarks left me wondering about the effect of his Catholic education. Why did he fail to hear or absorb the compassionate message of Jesus? I wondered how long it might take for him to believe and live what Thomas Kelly writes in *A Testament of Devotion*:

In the experience of the Divine Presence that which flows over the ocean of darkness is an infinite ocean of light and *love*. In the Eternal Now all people become seen in a new way. We enfold them in our love, and we and they are enfolded together within the great Love of God as we know it in Christ. . . . They aren't just masses of struggling beings, furthering or thwarting our ambitions, or, in far larger numbers, utterly alien to and insulated from us. We become identified with them and suffer when they suffer and rejoice when they rejoice. One might almost say we become cosmic mothers, tenderly caring for all.[7]

If those who *have* could become cosmic mothers, those who *have not* could regain their dignity and their rightful place among us.

REFLECTION

"Who are we to close doors? In the early church, even today there is the ministry of the ostiary [usher]. And what did the ostiary do? He opened the door, received the people, and allowed them to pass. But it was never the ministry of the closed door, never" (Pope Francis, *Morning Homilies III*).[8]

Have you ever experienced a "door" being closed to you by an individual or group? If so, what was that like for you?

PRAYER

Bring to mind one group of people on the margins with whom you sense discomfort. Picture yourself seated beside them at the banquet table with Jesus. Notice how welcoming he is toward everyone who is gathered there.

SCRIPTURE TO CARRY IN YOUR HEART TODAY

"How does God's love abide in anyone who has the world's goods and sees a brother or sister in need and yet refuses to help?" (1 Jn 3:17).

WEEK 4, DAY 2

THE TWO WOLVES IN US

Each of us has two wolves in the heart, one of love and one
of hate. Everything depends on which one we feed each day.

—Rick Hanson, *Buddha's Brain*[9]

One Sunday afternoon I glanced out the window and saw a young woman wearing an oversized, dirty black coat and baggy tan pants, a stocking cap on her head with black hair sticking out. She set down a plastic bag half-filled with cans for deposit refund and began rooting through the dumpster, opening up and shaking out garbage bags. After raking through them with her gloved hands, she took off the gloves, pulled newspapers out, and actually put her bare finger on her wet lips so she could easily turn the pages. I gasped, thinking of the ugly garbage she had just touched. As she discarded the newspapers, I realized she was looking for coupons. Remembering that some came in the mail a few days earlier, I found them—free coffee, two sandwiches for the price of one—clipped them together along with a twenty-dollar bill, and took them downstairs.

By the time I stepped outside, she had walked to the second dumpster at the end of the parking lot. I went over and asked as warmly as I could, "What brings you to this area?" She smiled in reply, "I'm staying with my uncle until I can get back on my feet again." I wondered about that but let it be and asked if she was looking for coupons. She seemed mildly surprised as I held them out to her. Then she saw the money and her eyes filled with tears. Next came *my* surprise. She instinctively reached out to hug me. I saw that gesture coming at the exact same time I looked at her garbage-smeared coat. In one brief second I pulled back, repulsed at the thought of getting that close to her. But in the next second I leaned in, not wanting to be offensive.

As I walked away with the distasteful aroma of garbage clinging to me, I thought of Jesus touching lepers without hesitation. I felt disappointed with myself for how quickly I wanted to draw back from someone on the margins of society. At the same time, I knew my hesitancy came from my brain's instinctual inclination to protect myself. I learned something vital in that brief space between repugnance and receptivity: I have a choice in how I respond to people, no matter how "other" they might appear to be. I have the ability to turn *toward*, rather than *away*. The more aware I am of the instinctual part of my brain that urges me to hide in the safety and security of "the tribe," the more compassionate and open I can choose to be in welcoming people who do not fit into that circle.

Neuropsychologist and meditation teacher Rick Hanson uses a familiar story to explain how tribalism, marginalization, and divisiveness are fostered. Hanson tells of someone asking a Native American grandmother what led to her being respected as a kindhearted, wise elder. She answered by saying that there were two wolves fighting within her, a wolf of love and a wolf of hate. She went on to explain that which wolf grew stronger would depend on the one she fed each day. The grandmother was obviously feeding the wolf of love.[10]

We probably have quite a few different types of wolves in us. The wolf is a metaphor of how we envision our relationship with humanity. For the *wolf of love* the view is wide and inclusive. The wolf of love finds expression in compassion, kindness, mercy, understanding, hospitality, justice, charity, and all the ways in which we approach others with a sincere desire of welcome and acceptance, regardless of a vast array of differences.

The *wolf of hate*, on the other hand, is a metaphor of the quick-snapping response that arises from a tribal sense of safety, security, loyalty, and protection. It guards "us" and reacts with fear and aggression against "them," snarls toward anyone posing a real or illusory threat. This wolf takes many forms, including prejudice, aggression, animosity, degradation, oppression, revenge, hostility, revulsion, humiliation, and any other response that judges and treats another human being as a threat or an enemy, viewing them as unequal and inferior.

Hanson explains that all humans have the propensity for love or hate. We cannot get rid of the wolf of hate, because it is a natural response of our instinctual, reptilian brain: "The wolf of hate is deeply embedded both in the human evolutionary past and in each person's brain today, ready to howl at any threat. . . . Acknowledging the wolf of hate prompts a very useful caution when you are in situations—arguing with neighbor, disciplining a child, reacting to criticism at work—in which you feel mistreated and revved up—and that wolf begins to stir."[11]

He concludes this explanation with a statement that carries both reality and caution: "Love and hate: they live and tumble together in every heart, like wolf cubs tussling in a cave. There is no killing the wolf of hate; the aversion in such an attempt would actually create what you're trying to destroy. But you can watch the wolf carefully, keep it tethered, and limit its alarm, righteousness, grievances, resentments, contempt and prejudice. Meanwhile, keep nourishing and encouraging the wolf of love."[12]

Fear, not hate, sparked my initial pulling back from the woman at the dumpster. My brain instantly warned me about the "disease" I could get from that gunk on her coat. Sometimes fear protects us, and we wisely follow its warning. In this case, the best and most loving response was to compassionately open my arms. Had I let the wolf of fear have its way, I never would have done that.

One more powerful example of not feeding the wolf of hate comes from an article by Benedictine monk Jerome Kodell. He recalled meeting a young man in the early 1960s who helped with voter registration during the civil rights movement. Kodell asked him if he had ever been hurt, and the young man replied, "I've been spit on, beaten with fists, with pipes, with chains and left a bloody mess." He told Kodell that at first he fought back, but then he realized he was adding to the hatred being spewed at him. He explained, "I decided I would not fight back. I would let my body absorb that hatred, so that some of it would die in my body and not bounce back into the world. I now see that my job in the midst of that evil is to make my body a grave for hate." Kodell concludes: "What he was describing was the gospel of Jesus. We do not fight evil with evil."[13]

REFLECTION

"God, in great longing for wholeness, constantly invites us to dismantle all that is exclusive. We cannot be whole until we come to embrace all that God has made and to share all that God has given. In matters and issues of exclusion we may be sure that God is always on the outside with those very people whom we do not accept" (Edwina Gateley, *A Mystical Heart*).[14]

How do you experience the wolf of love and the wolf of hate in yourself?

PRAYER

Visualize the wolf of love and the wolf of hate in your heart. Imagine that Jesus stands by your side as you speak to each of the wolves about your life.

SCRIPTURE TO CARRY IN YOUR HEART TODAY

"You have heard that it was said, 'An eye for an eye and a tooth for a tooth.' But I say to you, Do not resist an evildoer. But if anyone strikes you on the right cheek, turn the other also" (Mt 5:38–39).

WEEK 4, DAY 3

FAR FROM THE TREE

An intolerance of diversity is the
biggest threat to peace in our times.
—Vandana Shiva, *Earth Democracy*[15]

There's a saying, when speaking about children who resemble their parents, that "the apple does not fall far from the tree." However, children with disabilities often fall miles from the tree—and often suffer the consequences for much of their life. Andrew Solomon interviewed more than three hundred families who parented children born with conditions such as autism, dwarfism, transgenderism, deafness, Down syndrome, and schizophrenia. "It never occurred to me, not even in my wildest disaster scenarios, that I would have a child different enough to elicit stares and change the way I think about a trip to the store or a walk on the beach," said one mother. Another parent commented, "Compassion is the ability to care unconditionally for another person, not based on fulfilling your expectations." Other parents had similar responses, yet most of them said they would not change their experience—even though parenting a child with special needs requires exceptional energy and patient dedication.[16]

Unfortunately, society still exhibits great discomfort toward people with disabilities. We have not been taught how to relate compassionately to those who are "different" from what we consider to be the "normal way to look and act." A tendency to feel uncomfortable and act in a condescending or patronizing manner still persists. Mentally and physically challenged adults in L'Arche communities have often experienced this attitude. The founder of L'Arche, Jean Vanier, tells the story of an exceedingly sad man who came to visit about his numerous problems at home and work. Vanier thought the man probably considered himself to be a very "normal" person. As the man was speaking, Jean Claude, who has Down syndrome, burst into the office. He laughed the whole time while he continually shook hands with Vanier and the visitor. As Jean Claude left the office laughing, the visitor looked at Vanier and remarked, "Isn't it sad that there are children like that?" In reflecting on the experience, Vanier commented:

> The great pain in all of this is that the man was totally blind. He had barriers inside of him and was unable to see that Jean Claude was happy. . . . Fundamentally, when people start lamenting because there are people with handicaps in our world, the question is whether it is more sad that there are people with handicaps or that there are people who reject them. Which is the greater handicap? Is it that there are men like Jean Claude or is it that Mr. Normal has this barrier which renders him totally blind to the beauty of people?[17]

In an Internet video, "A Credo for Support," adults with mental and physical challenges ask that they be given "equity and respect," and that people do not try to fix them (an attitude implying they are broken). In a long list of appeals, they request to be seen as "a friend, a fellow citizen, and a neighbor," rather than treated as a detached "client." The statement at the opening of the video describes how cruelly adults with mental and physical disabilities have been marginalized: "Throughout history, people with disabilities have been abandoned at birth, banished from society, used as court jesters, drowned and burned during the Inquisition, gassed in Nazi Germany, and still continue to be segregated, institutionalized, tortured in the name of behavior management, abused, raped, euthanized, and murdered."[18]

Marginalization unfortunately takes place within every sphere of humanity. Bryan Stevenson tells heartbreaking stories in *Just Mercy* as he demonstrates how those judged as "criminals" are human beings, each with their own story. Their life situations reveal why they end up in prison, many of them unfairly placed there due to skin color or lack of compassionate advocacy. When a prisoner's story is known, we may be less likely to think we are "better than" him or her. For example, what if our early years had been like Trina's, who suffered horrific childhood trauma and developed mental illness due to a raging father who regularly beat her mother senseless and sexually assaulted her daughters? Trina eventually fled that hellish place and lived on the streets until convicted as a young teenager of accidentally setting a house fire that resulted in several deaths. Due to Pennsylvania law, Trina was sentenced to life in prison without parole, even though the judge acknowledged she had "no intent to kill."[19]

When any person or group is regarded as lesser than others who consider themselves superior, marginalization occurs. This attitude shows in both subtle and obvious ways. John Lewis points to this as the main reason for society's struggles. He advocates dispelling "the erroneous, pervasive, and persistent belief that we are somehow separated from the divine, that some of us have more light than others, therefore making them more deserving than others." As long as we believe "some people are more special, more beautiful, more capable, more influential, more intelligent, more gifted, and have a greater capacity for good than others, often based on material possessions and outer appearances," marginalization will continue unabated.[20]

When he was interviewed by Krista Tippett on National Public Radio, Jean Vanier pointed to the wide divide of marginalization and added another cause for its occurrence.

> We don't know what to do with our own weakness except hide it or pretend it doesn't exist. So how can we welcome fully the weakness of another, if we haven't welcomed our own weakness? There are very strong words of Martin Luther King. His question was always, how is it that one group—the white group—can despise the other group, which is the black group? And will it always be like this? Will we always be having an elite condemning or pushing down others that they consider not worthy? And he says something I find extremely beautiful and strong, that we will continue to despise people until we have recognized, loved and accepted what is despicable in ourselves.[21]

We each fall "far from the tree." None of us is perfectly shaped in body, mind, and spirit. None of us conforms to some magical ideal of how every human ought to be. We each have our own disability and differences. When we know this, our compassion can reach out extensively.

REFLECTION

"Too often we reject people in their weaknesses; we refuse those with needs different from our own needs; we have no time for the poor or weak person. We are embarrassed by the weak and we seek to avoid them because we cannot accept or believe that this weak person is God and God is here in this weak flesh" (Ilia Delio, *Compassion: Living in the Spirit of St. Francis*).[22]

What would you name as your weaknesses and vulnerability? How do these affect your approach and attitude toward people with disabilities?

PRAYER

Compassionate One, help me to keep an open heart toward each person, no matter how different they appear to be. Increase my desire to welcome each one with your compassion.

SCRIPTURE TO CARRY IN YOUR HEART TODAY

"Blessed are the poor in spirit, for theirs is the kingdom of heaven" (Mt 5:3).

WEEK 4, DAY 4

REMOVING THE BOULDERS

*Moreover, compassion is dangerous because it
often challenges the status quo and the socially
entrenched values that support it.*

—Maureen O'Connell, *Compassion*[23]

In this age of globalization, the weight of oppressive poverty and the social ills of injustice press like enormous boulders on a multitude of people. Large corporations, economic systems, political alignments, precipitous climate changes, and other global influences significantly affect everyone on our planet, but particularly those who are impoverished. Much can be done by compassionate care and personal presence to alleviate the afflictions and distress of world citizens whose lives are underprivileged, but that is not enough. We must also become knowledgeable about the forces that push the boulders onto these people and take action to remove them.

Because I am a planetary citizen and not simply an individual existing independently from everyone else, my life is connected with countless strangers living on other parts of Earth. The cell phone I use contains minerals from dark, dank mines in Africa where young children labor; I wear clothes that women in Sri Lanka create by working in unsafe factory conditions. Many of the foods I eat arrive from distant lands where subsistence farmers grow and harvest the food for inadequate pay. I fly in airplanes whose use of fossil fuels produces carbon that pollutes the atmosphere in faraway places. Every gesture of my day touches the larger community of this world in some way. And yet, I can easily disregard this reality and the reasons for why I live a privileged life, while most of the world never experiences my benefits.

Fordham University professor Maureen O'Connell addresses this issue by inviting her readers to enter the arena of compassionate action. According to O'Connell, "Loving our suffering neighbor in a global age demands that we recognize how unjust suffering unites three-quarters of the world's population." She proposes that "we scrutinize our connections to this suffering, and in particular the ways in which our privilege acts to prevent us from doing so." O'Connell insists that we not only become aware of our connection to how others suffer but that we respond to our fallen neighbors as the Good Samaritan did in the gospel parable. We are to commit ourselves to actively "create new relationships with the capacity to transform ourselves and the social reality."[24]

O'Connell affirms the goodness of people who contribute financially to organizations working for justice in times of crisis. She also challenges these actions as being insufficient, asking if people who contribute at a distance—"click on the internet, give, and forget"—also ensure that those victimized by social injustice have access to "long-term health care, decent education, affordable housing, or meaningful work." Dr. Martin Luther King Jr. termed this action of never getting directly involved "compassion by proxy." O'Connell calls it "cultural amnesia," an approach that "demands little of us" and prevents us from acknowledging and remembering our responsibility.[25]

Monetary donations serve to keep compassionate nonprofits afloat and active, so this form of contributing ought not be disregarded or downplayed. At the same time, it is all too easy to sit back and think our compassionate response suffices once we have donated financially. Education toward greater awareness is vital because knowledge of the world's suffering and its causes can move us toward action. Access to a wide variety of resources with information concerning injustice lies at our fingertips. A bit of searching on the Internet opens up a world of valuable websites and articles: Network, Bread for the World, TED talks, and so on. Still, we may unconsciously resist knowing the facts about suffering on our planet and our part in its causation.

In *Justice Rising,* John Heagle brushes aside discouragement as he reflects on the factors driving "classism, racism, sexism, war." Heagle offers hope for lessening the "powers of oppression" through "education, social resistance, solidarity and programs of opportunity." Like O'Connell, he teaches the need for directing attention to injustice from the perspective of our own terrain: "We are called to name the sources of oppression in our institutions, to unmask the injustice in our religious structures, and to engage the violence in our political systems." Heagle also reminds the reader of the support to be gleaned in the Catholic Church's encyclicals on social justice in which the Church adds "its voice to the concerns surrounding world markets, justice for the poor, and the need for a more just economic vision."[26]

When Heagle determines the causes of global injustice, he identifies "the system of empire" as a central cause. He then delineates six characteristics of this empire: (1) a hierarchical type of authority; (2) a presumption of inequalities being the norm in the way resources are shared; (3) a requirement of having enemies and an atmosphere of insecurity, based on fear and suspicion of the "other"; (4) war as the way the structures of the empire are promoted and protected; (5) religious institutions legitimizing the vision and practice of the empire regarding war; and (6) peace, defined as the interval between wars, based on competition, domination, and triumph.[27]

The work of dismantling the system of the empire includes attentiveness to our own interior transformation. In Heagle's words, we must have "a willingness to die to our learned cultural preference for control, and to let go of the collective attitudes of racism, greed, gender bias, homophobia, and other forms of prejudice."[28]

There is much to be done.

REFLECTION

"If each kept only what is required for his [or her] current needs, and left the surplus for the needy, wealth and poverty would be abolished. . . . The bread you keep belongs to another who is starving, the coat that lies in your chest is stolen from the naked, the shoes that rot in your house are stolen from the person who goes unshod, the money you laid aside is stolen from the poverty-stricken. In this way, you are the oppressors of as many people as you could help. No, it is not your rapaciousness that is condemned, but your refusal to share" (St. Basil the Great).

What do you own that could be given away? How might you go about doing this?

PRAYER

Guardian of Oppressed People, the weight of repressive poverty can be eased if persons like myself help to bear the burden. Turn my eyes, my heart, and my hands in their direction.

SCRIPTURE TO CARRY IN YOUR HEART TODAY

"All who believed were together and had all things in common; they would sell their possessions and goods and distribute the proceeds to all, as any had need" (Acts 2:44–45).

WEEK 4, DAY 5

CULTIVATING RELATIONSHIPS

*Universal peace can only come if we develop
and awaken the capacity to love people, to respect them
deeply, to live authentic relationships with others, to yearn
for truth and justice in the huge family of humanity.*

—Jean Vanier, Templeton Award Speech[29]

Relationships nurture compassion and help it to thrive. When we feel empathy for someone who suffers, we immediately establish a connection with that person. I've carried on extended correspondence with incarcerated people, a man suffering from schizophrenia, a homeless woman, and others whom I will probably never meet in person. I feel a kinship with them; they have allowed me into a part of their lives and deepened my empathy by trusting me to see the world from their perspectives.

For five years I met every Monday afternoon with Maria, the daughter of undocumented immigrants. Reading Maureen O'Connell's *Compassion* had nudged me to go beyond excuses of having "an overly full schedule," "too much travel," or "I wouldn't know what to do." So I joined a volunteer program where children from low-income families receive community support and assistance for their educational development. The first time I met with Maria, she was a thin, extremely shy eight-year-old. Today, this confident young woman stands tall and has become a gifted writer. Maria taught me so much about the value of relationships as we sat side by side, week after week, developing her language skills.

The more I came to know this dear child and her family, the more I empathized with those who leave homeland, relatives, language, and culture to settle in a new country where one is viewed with suspicion and enmity. My relationship with Maria taught me about the hidden suffering her family experienced. I realized in a keener way that when we have no connection or relationship with people who are different from ourselves, it is much easier to lack concern for what happens to them. We must be willing to invest ourselves in actual relationships with marginalized persons. Empathy develops when we know another's personal history.

Sister of Mercy Marilyn Lacey attests to the power and value of compassionate relationships in her extensive ministry with refugees in Africa, Asia, Eastern Europe, and Latin America. Throughout *This Flowing toward Me,* Lacey's reflections reveal the dignity and respect she gives to each person she serves and the loving-kindness she receives from them. Her recognition of God's tenderness toward the refugees she aids shines on each page. One cannot help but develop a fondness for the people whom she loves:

> In my own interaction with refugees, I have experienced a God who sits with the abandoned, who weeps with the sorrowing, who encourages those on the verge of losing all hope. I know the God who walks—no, limps with the poor. I have met this God in refugees who share their meager rations of water with passers-by. I have heard God in the songs they sing into the desert night. I have stood beside God at graveside vigils for those who died of a scorpion bite or malaria. I have seen God in the eyes of child soldiers convinced their deeds are unforgivable.
>
> This God lives in "hiddenness" and seeks the lowest place. This God knows helplessness and sorrow and collects the tears of those who grieve. This God is

all too familiar with neglect and confinement and failure. This God stands solidly against injustice, yet refuses all forms of violence. This God's face is mercy.[30]

Nobel Peace Prize winner Wangari Maathai—a member of
the Kenyan Kikuyu tribe—discovered the necessity of establishing relationships in her compassionate decision to replant trees
in her badly deforested country. The land suffered greatly from
erosion due to barrenness, causing the nutritional topsoil to be
washed away, so Maathai set out to plant trees. Without the aid
of local people to water and tend them, however, the seedlings
perished. In time, Maathai realized her error in trying to carry
out her dream alone. She tried again. This time she taught the
women in villages the importance of trees as a protective wa-
tershed on their fields and their value as shade, fuel, and food.
Maathai organized the villages into groups to care for the plant-
ings and be given a small fee for every tree that lived. In this
way she acknowledged the dignity of the women and helped
them feel valued for assisting in protecting the land. Through
these relationships, Wangari Maathai's dream of planting thirty
million trees came true.[31]

Compassionate presence thrives on trusted relationships. A
friend and I wanted to help support women living in a halfway
house after their incarceration ended. After several meetings
with the housing director, we planned a day-long retreat. Only
two women came, and they had to be coaxed there by the staff.
Why? Because none of the women had a relationship with us.
Their life experiences resulted in a low trust level. The women
feared risking their presence to people they did not know.

Using *the* to identify groups of people keeps them at a distance and negates a relationship with them. Naming people as
the poor, *the* diabetic in Room 214, *the* alcoholic, or *the* homeless
snips off the thread of connection. People become objectified

rather than personalized. When we do not have a connection with a person or group, it becomes much easier to demonize or scapegoat them for the ills of society. Marginalized people know this from experience. Fr. Joe Nassal tells of an evening when he stopped to buy a newspaper from a homeless person. They had a few minutes' conversation. As he moved on, Fr. Nassal thanked the man. He responded, "Oh, no, it's you I need to thank. I've been here nine hours, and you're the first one to look me in the eye."

REFLECTION

What do you most enjoy about your relationships with persons to whom you extend compassion?

PRAYER

Welcoming One, draw me close to those who are marginalized when I want to keep my distance. Lead me into relationships with persons whom society pushes to the edge. Nudge me with your grace when I hesitate in extending hospitality to others.

SCRIPTURE TO CARRY IN YOUR HEART TODAY

"I was a stranger and you welcomed me" (Mt 25:35).

WEEK 4, DAY 6

HAVE YOU LOVED WELL?

I was hungry and you gave me food, I was thirsty and you gave
me something to drink, I was a stranger and you welcomed me,
I was naked and you gave me clothing, I was sick and you took
care of me, I was in prison and you visited me.

—Matthew 25:35–36

The verses opening this page come from a parable Jesus used to teach what will be of most value at the end of our life. The Church has long named these verses the Corporal Works of Mercy, but that is a misnomer. The deeds in the parable are actually the Works of Compassion. *Mercy*, according to Webster's Dictionary, means "forgiveness shown toward someone whom it is within one's power to punish or harm." Mercy, therefore, has a specific intent. It is one aspect of compassion, as are sympathy, justice, charity, kindness, and other related qualities. They all dwell in the house of compassion.

The actions given in the parable of Matthew 25 include both reality and metaphor. They do not contain all the deeds for extending compassion. Rather, they point to what St. John of the Cross indicated as the most vital question at the end of our life: "Have you loved well? Was everything that was done, done for love's sake?"[32] Did we reach beyond ourselves to those who suffered and were in need? Did we let go of a sense of entitlement or privilege and recognize how much we could give? Were we generous with our gifts and cognizant of Christ's presence within the persons whom our compassionate works benefited?

The heart of Christian service dwells in the line that follows the deeds of compassion that Jesus named in the parable: "Just as you did it to one of the least of these who are members of my family, you did it to me" (Mt 25:40). When our compassionate deeds resemble those of the parable, we reveal the face of the Holy One. We make visible the hiddenness of Christ with our actions when they come from the storehouse of our love. This manifestation of divine life within us enlivens our compassionate service.

Both Mother Teresa, founder of the Missionaries of Charity, and Dorothy Day, founder of the Catholic Worker movement, spoke of Christ in "his distressing disguise." They received spiritual energy from this concept of faith. Mother Teresa reminded her community: "More than ever people want to see love in action through our humble works—how necessary it is for us to be in love with Jesus—to be able to feed Him in the hungry and the lonely."[33] Dorothy Day wrote: "Christ is always with us, always asking for room in our hearts. . . . He made heaven hinge on the way we act toward Him in His disguise of commonplace, frail, ordinary humanity."[34]

When I reflect on the gospel accounts of Jesus touching the lives of those who came into his presence, I marvel at the kindness that flowed from him. I imagine what it must have been like to stand nearby, to receive his smile of acceptance, his look of forgiveness, his hand of healing. How is it that through all these years the power of this beloved presence continues to touch hearts in such a dramatic way? The kindness of Christ continues to thrive through the ages because we each bear this love within us. We give and receive compassion within the blessed circle of this divine presence in whom "we live and move and have our being" (Acts 17:26).

Jean Vanier gives both encouragement and challenge as he describes the suffering around us that requires our attention and assistance. One can almost hear in Vanier's words those of Jesus in the parable of Matthew 25:

There are many hungry people in our world. God is not going to send down some bread from the trees, because if somebody is hungry, it's our problem. If somebody is sick, it's my problem; it's your problem. If somebody is closed up in an institution because he has a disability, it's my problem. We have to do something about it. If people have a toothache, you don't just pray for him or her, you take them to a good dentist. And Jesus says to us, "It's up to you to do something about it, but I give you my spirit. I'll give you a new force, a new strength, and a new wisdom so that you can break down the dividing walls of hostility." It's up to you and me, but God will give us strength if we open our hearts to him and ask for that strength.[35]

We incarnate the Works of Compassion when we serve food at a homeless shelter, bring our clothing to a St. Vincent de Paul store, counsel the distressed, care for a medical patient, welcome immigrants into our neighborhood, teach students kindheartedly, take time to listen to someone's troubles, stop by to visit aging or grieving individuals, write to prisoners, or sit by the bedside of the ill and dying. Whenever we are reaching beyond our own interests to those whose life could benefit from our kindness, we are responding yes to that most vital of all questions: "Have you loved well?"

REFLECTION

Reread the Works of Compassion in Matthew 25:35–36. Which ones most reflect your compassionate actions? Which ones least reflect your compassionate actions? Is there one of these works that you might focus on today?

PRAYER

Companion of Those Who Are Marginalized, thank you for stirring your love in my heart. I intend to act with loving-kindness, remembering that you are dwelling within each person. Each face I see today will be a reflection of you.

SCRIPTURE TO CARRY IN YOUR HEART TODAY

"Just as you did it to one of the least of these who are members of my family, you did it to me" (Mt 25:40).

WEEK 4, DAY 7

REVIEW AND REST

The Lord wants us to belong to a Church that knows
how to open her arms and welcome everyone, that is,
not a house for a few, but a house for everyone,
where all can be renewed, transformed, sanctified
by his love—the strongest and the weakest, sinners, the
indifferent, those who feel discouraged or lost.

—Pope Francis, *The Church of Mercy*[36]

Choose any or all of the following as a way to review Week Four:

- What three aspects of "From Hostility to Hospitality" were of greatest significance to you this past week?

- Do you think or feel any differently about marginalized persons after this week's reflections?

- What stands out for you as most helpful in lessening the great divide between *haves* and *have nots*?

- Reflect on how you lived this week. What are some ways that you "loved well" through one or more of the Works of Compassion?

- Which day's reflection challenged you the most?

- Which one left you nodding your head yes?

- As you look back over the week, were there moments or situations that awakened a fuller understanding of what it means to be marginalized?

- Draw a circle. On the outer edge of the circle, write the names of individuals and groups that you tend to marginalize. Then, slowly, intentionally and prayerfully, write your name next to any of the names that you are willing to join there on the margin.

- Browse through the daily news. Pause by each story of someone, or some group, that experiences marginalization. Ask yourself: "What do I think and how do I feel about this person or group? What would it be like if I opened my heart and welcomed any or all of these persons whose stories I am reading?"

WEEK FIVE

A THOUSAND UNBREAKABLE LINKS

INTRODUCTION

No matter what world we live in now, we are
all people of the earth, connected to one
another by our mutual humanity.

—Angeles Arrien, *The Four-Fold Way*[1]

When primatologist Jane Goodall was interviewed in 2013, she referred to a scientific discovery showing the extraordinary ability of Earth and humans to sustain life. She spoke about "the scientists who drilled down into the permafrost and brought up the remains of an Ice Age squirrel's nest. In the plant material, they found three living cells and from those living cells they managed to recreate the plant, which was a meadow's wheat. It's 32,000 years old, but it's now growing and seeding and reproducing. That's the resilience of nature, the incredible human brain, and the indomitable human spirit."[2]

When humans and nature are in sync with one another, amazing things happen. When they are out of touch or imbalanced, disastrous things occur. We are at a point in human history when this intimate relationship has become increasingly out of sync. With this inconsistency comes an ever-greater amount of suffering for our planet.

Compassion includes *all* of life. Humans are not the only receptors of our empathy. We owe our kindness to each and every part of what makes up our environment. The water and inhabitants of our immense oceans, the soil on our rich farmlands and our mineral-filled mountainsides, and the forests and creatures dwelling within them, from the tiniest to the tallest, from the strongest to the most fragile—there exists nothing that is unworthy of the touch of our compassionate, protective care.

In the coming days, I invite you to reflect on the tremendous gift we have in being citizens of Earth, to enter the wonder of our dwelling on this exceedingly generous home in the cosmos. I encourage you to gaze upon the ways that nature and spirituality companion one another. I ask you to become more aware of the growing need to have empathy for the suffering inflicted on Earth by human consumption, indifference, and greed. My hope is that this week will enable you to take a more encompassing look at how much gratitude we owe our planet, and that it will inspire you to renew a desire to care well for this vulnerable home of ours.

Each piece of creation intertwines. The suffering of one part of life touches all the other parts. Poet Mary Oliver reminds us: "I would say that there exist a thousand unbreakable links between each of us and everything else, and that our dignity and our chances are one. The farthest star and the mud at our feet are a family; and there is no decency or sense in honoring one thing, or a few things, and then closing the list. The pine tree, the leopard, the Platte River, and ourselves—we are at risk together, or we are on our way to a sustainable world together. We are each other's destiny."[3]

We are most surely "each other's destiny." We may sometimes feel separated and distant from the rest of creation, but this denies the reality. We cannot take a sip of water or tie a shoelace without having done so because of some aspect of Earth providing for us. When we enlarge our awareness of this interdependence, our spirits respond with wonderment and appreciation for so intimate a relationship.

Let us look more keenly at what we have failed or forgotten to notice about the suffering of our planet and the causes of that pain. Let us step further into our efforts to care responsibly for Earth and be grateful for how we grow closer to the Holy One when we attune to the natural world. Let us wake up to being fully alive.

Andrew Harvey's study of Rumi's poetry led him to trust that aliveness, and to insist on the openness we need: "If your soul is closed, you have no sense of the immense aliveness of everything." He then goes on to explain that when we look at a deeper level, if we look intuitively at the inherent mystery dwelling within life, we will see much more than is apparent to the naked eye:

> When you see the Divine world and look at a blade of grass, you see the swarming in light of millions of atoms; you see the atoms dancing, you experience the ecstatic connection between you and the blade of grass, and you see that the entire universe is danc- ing inside the blade of grass. There is nothing that is not totally alive. The rocks are dancing, everything is dancing. [As Rumi notes,] "Never think the earth is void or dead" because that is the fatal illusion, that is what enables us to exploit and rape nature.[4]

Our planet breathes with vitality. Let us do all we can to keep that breath of life robust and healthy.

WEEK 5, DAY 1

LIVING ON PLANET EARTH

In our day, a new awareness of the magnificence of
Earth as a small planet hospitable to life is growing
among peoples everywhere. This living planet, with its
thin spherical shell of land, water, and breathable air,
is our home, our only home in the vast universe.

—Elizabeth Johnson, *Ask the Beasts*[5]

If ever there was an artist who appreciates the beauty of Earth and empathizes with the planet's pain, it is Mary Southard, C.S.J. One of my favorite paintings is the one that she painted of a boy lying on his back; his bent arms rest comfortably behind his head. He is stretched out on the curve of our planet, looking, not *up*, but *out* into a space filled with planets and stars. The boy's serene posture and calm face imply a oneness with what he observes. Until I reflected on this painting, I never really appreciated the astonishing fact that I am looking *out* to the cosmos, not just *up* to it. I am encompassed by the universe when I gaze outward from Earth toward the "heavens."[6]

Southard's painting reminds me that I am a native, not only of Earth, but of the vast universe—our ancient planet's birthplace. According to scientific studies, Earth developed more than 4.5 billion years ago from a gaseous explosion in space. How this planet came to be a hospitable residence for life remains a fact incredible to comprehend—as does our intimate union with not only every particle of our planet, but with the universe as well. Astrophysicist Neil deGrasse Tyson reminds us: "We are part of this universe; we are in this universe, but perhaps more important than both of those facts, is that the universe is in us." Each cell of ours is composed of substance from our planet, the substance created from the cosmic star that birthed Earth into form.[7]

Not long after I became familiar with Mary Southard's painting, I traveled to Dorking, England. During this visit, my hosts took me to a park with a green hillside. I climbed the high hill, lay down on my back, stretched out, and put my arms behind my head like the boy in the painting. As I lay there, I felt completely at peace and in wonderment at being on the curve of Earth, gazing outward into space. I often return to that profound and joyful experience with a grateful sense of Earth's carrying me through the Milky Way galaxy.

The more I perceive the reality of my actually living among the universe, the more I appreciate the miracle of living on a planet that not only stays in orbit, but generates life in abundance. I like to imagine what it must be like for astronauts to see this blue-green globe floating and rotating gracefully in space. Sally Ride, the first female USA astronaut, described it this way:

> The view of Earth is absolutely spectacular, and the feeling of looking back and seeing your planet as a planet is just an amazing feeling. It's a totally different perspective, and it makes you appreciate, actually, how fragile our existence is. You can look at Earth's horizon and see this really, really thin royal blue line right along the horizon, and at first you don't really quite internalize what that is, and then you realize that it's Earth's atmosphere, and that that's all there is of it, and it's about as thick as the fuzz on a tennis ball, and it's everything that separates us from the vacuum of space.[8]

"As thick as the fuzz on a tennis ball." Those words of Sally Ride's both impress me and startle me. I want to shout to everyone about the vulnerable and remarkable sphere on which we have the privilege to dwell. I believe humans would more readily extend kindness to our planet if they were acutely aware of how precious this place truly is.

Earth pulses—generously creating, nurturing, and sustaining diverse life. Judy Cannato points to the wonder of our planet as a biological organism in its own right, one with a self-regulating ecosystem: "Earth has maintained a steady surface temperature over hundreds of millions of years, just as any biological organism does. Also, salt in Earth's seas remains below the saturation point so that the oceans do not become lethal to plant and animal life, in spite of the fact that each year tons of salt run off into the seas. . . . Rain forests act as lungs and rivers as arteries. Earth is alive, an organism with systems that support her life and ours."[9] This self-regulating system is now changing, and at a dangerous speed. Humans are throwing Earth's natural lifesaving processes off balance, to the peril of every inhabitant. As long as humans keep their distance and view Earth as an inanimate object, there will be little inspiration to care well for this living body.

The closer we come to the natural world by spending intentional time there, the more we come to know our planet as the wondrous abode it is. The closer we observe and absorb the wonder of such precious gifts as the fragrance of flowers, the fresh air of a rain shower, the delicate flight of a butterfly, the sound of strong ocean waves, the persistent song of a wren, or the cavorting leaps of young foxes, the more tender our appreciation will be for what we have been given.

We are temporary occupants on this magnificent planet that supports life, a planet that thrives and responds positively when humans respect that life. While we live here, let us do our part to end destructive habits that inhibit the sustaining gifts of our beautiful Earth, the place we call home.

REFLECTION

Stand and look at the cosmos that's visible to you—the sky, sun, moon, or stars—remaining silent and contemplating this with a reverent gaze. Remember where you stand: on the curve of an astounding orb floating through the universe. Bow deeply in respect for what you behold.

PRAYER

"Limitless love, from the depths to the stars: flooding all, loving all. It is the royal kiss of peace" (St. Hildegard of Bingen).

Boundless Love, you flow through the cosmos and extend your limitless compassion to every particle. I pray today that your kiss of peace will touch each part of our planet that suffers due to human actions.

SCRIPTURE TO CARRY IN YOUR HEART TODAY

"The heavens are telling the glory of God;

and the firmament proclaims [God's] handiwork.

Day to day pours forth speech,

and night to night declares knowledge.

There is no speech, nor are there words;

their voice is not heard;

yet their voice goes out through all the earth,

and their words to the end of the world." (Ps 19:1–4)

WEEK 5, DAY 2

DIFFERENT THAN, NOT BETTER THAN

Deep ecology recognizes that nothing short of a total revolution in consciousness will be of lasting use in preserving the life-support systems of our planet.

—Joanna Macy et al., *Thinking like a Mountain*[10]

During the mid-1970s, when I joined a group studying Elizabeth Dodson Gray's *Green Paradise Lost,* I gained a life-changing insight. After years of education in Catholic schools and well into my twenties, I'd assumed that humans were superior to the rest of creation. Much of this belief rested on several biblical texts, including the narrative of creation in the book of Genesis: "Be fruitful and multiply, and fill the earth and *subdue it*; and *have dominion* over the fish of the sea and over the birds of the air and over every living thing that moves upon the earth" (Gn 1:28–29; emphasis added). Psalm 8 also echoes these words, as does the apocryphal book of Sirach (see Sir 17:1–4).

A profoundly new way of thinking evolved for me when Elizabeth Dodson Gray suggested viewing creation with the lens of "different than," instead of "better than." This theory unraveled my belief of being superior to nonhuman life. I could no longer treat the natural world with a hierarchical attitude. I became aware that each piece of creation has its own sacredness and reason for existence. My human brain and bodily system have a more developed complexity, but this does not give me the right to "subdue" anyone or anything. I am to value and treat kindly what the Creator repeatedly calls "good" in the story of creation (see Gn 1:1–31). This, of course, means *all* of existence. The domination theory has been with us for centuries and roots itself deeply in the human psyche. No wonder people act as if they can destroy in nature whatever they fear or consider inconvenient or of no use.

One summer I directed a retreat at a lovely spirituality center with a new pond nearby. The first evening a symphony of various kinds of frogs croaked and "ribbeted" in the water, lulling me to sleep. Imagine my surprise the next morning when one of the participants approached me angrily, asking, "What was that horrible sound coming from outside all night?" After I explained, she demanded, "You've got to get rid of them. Can't you just kill them?"

Everything has a right to exist. When something in nature threatens to destroy or hurt us, we need to protect ourselves, but this does not mean we eliminate something because of a remote possibility of harm. In a Guatemalan forest, I came across a big tarantula in front of me. I had never seen one, and I gulped with fear. Then I stepped back and walked far around the creature. Many years later I heard a moving poem by Faith Shearin in which she describes her daughter trying to convince her to buy a tarantula. She tells her mother some reasons why they are good pets: tarantulas keep their burrows tidy and dry; they're gentle and try hard not to bite; they fling their hairs to protect themselves. (I learned a lot from that poem).[11]

We ought not to practice dominion over anything, not even tiny organisms. Each has value. As soon as people see a honey bee nearby, they often want to swat and kill it. But without bees to pollinate blossoms, we would not have future fruits and vegetables. Consider how some people never give a second thought to getting rid of earthworms. These silent residents of the soil greatly improve the soil's fertility by converting various kinds of matter into enriching humus. If you find earthworms in a garden, you have found a treasure.

Scientist Carl Safina's studies of the cognitive and emotional behavior of animals reveals further motivation for humans to end the false belief of being superior to the rest of creation. Safina's extensive research shows that wolves, killer whales, chimps, elephants, and other creatures have emotional responses not all that different from humans—such as empathy, jealousy, maternal love, friendship, and grief.[12] Not long after I read Safina's *Beyond Words: What Animals Think and Feel*, I viewed a PBS series that included a program on the maternal instincts of nonhumans. That study left me deeply touched with the beauty of how these mothers tenderly care for their young. I marveled at the scene of an enormous alligator taking her newborns down to the water by opening her wide mouth with its large, sharp teeth and scooping the babies in without hurting them.

Studies of trees also demonstrate that humans are not the only ones with the ability to think and be compassionate. Scientists in Germany learned how trees help one another to grow through their connected root systems. When individual trees grow in the same area but live on varied soil (some on rocky ground, others on nutritious dirt), the rate of photosynthesis produces the same amount of sugar for the leaves of both healthy and more vulnerable trees. The stronger trees take less nutrients so the others can have more. Trees obviously have their own form of empathic kindness.[13]

Trees also protect themselves and their neighbors by communicating with each other. When giraffes on the African savanna stroll by and start eating leaves on the acacia trees, the acacias quickly give off ethylene gas, which giraffes dislike. This scent travels to nearby acacias to warn them about the predator. Pine trees do much the same when beetles start boring into their bark. The pines know to protect themselves by releasing resin onto their bark so the beetles cannot bore through it. Like the acacias, the pines also compassionately emit a fragrance to alert other pines nearby to protect themselves. Research shows that "the leaf tissue sends out electrical signals, just as human tissue does when it is hurt in some way."[14]

Information such as this confirms that nonhumans have their own types of intelligence and communication. They too know about empathy and suffering. We humans will do well to step down from our pedestals of presumed power and reach out with benevolent respect to our fellow inhabitants of planet Earth.

REFLECTION

What part of creation do you find most difficult to consider being your sister or brother? What would it take for you to change this emotional response?

PRAYER

Lover of All Life, thank you for each part of creation. Release my mind and heart from a desire to think of myself as better than nonhumans. Keep teaching me how to open my mind and heart to all of life.

SCRIPTURE TO CARRY IN YOUR HEART TODAY

"But ask the animals, and they will teach you; the birds of the air, and they will tell you;

ask the plants of the earth, and they will teach you; and the fish of the sea will declare to you." (Job 12:7–8)

WEEK 5, DAY 3

ALL CREATION GROANS

All creation, together as a whole, awaits freedom
from bondage. All creation groans for wholeness
and stretches forward in transformation.

—Judy Cannato, *Radical Amazement*[15]

As I walked along the fields near a retreat center in rural Nebraska one early spring day, my heart leapt for joy. I was thrilled to hear a western meadowlark's lovely song. The melody took me back immediately to my farm days when their plentiful songs filled the air. Sighting them now is a rarity. Like so many other wonder-full creatures on our planet, they are losing the capacity to survive.

In the opening pages of *Ask the Beasts*, Elizabeth Johnson states the situation facing our planet today: "For all our abilities, *Homo sapiens* is ravaging the world of life. Although some prefer to remain blind with denial, the fact is we have crossed a threshold into a new moment of human history dangerous to the well-being of the diversity of life on this planet."[16]

We do not have to look far to see how the natural world suffers. The pain of our planet becomes visible in polluted waters failing to support life, destroyed rainforests that cannot contribute life-giving oxygen, land stripped of its precious topsoil to build shopping malls, carbon-polluted air damaging our preciously thin layer of atmosphere, the elimination of wildlife habitats, and the extinction of species of animals, plants, insects, reptiles, and microorganisms. In *Laudato Si'*, Pope Francis's encyclical on the environment, he writes, "The pace of consumption, waste and environmental change has so stretched the planet's capacity that our contemporary lifestyle, unsustainable as it is, can only precipitate catastrophes."[17]

Disregard and unawareness often lead to environmental harm. Something as basic as the food we choose to eat, or not to eat, creates a significant impact. "Have you ever taken a good look, a really good look, at what you're throwing out in your kitchen garbage?" writes Letitia Star.

> The EPA estimates that every year the average family of four tosses two million calories, costing about $1,500. The USDA reports that a whopping thirty-one percent of our food (133 billion pounds) is trashed. Such statistics don't take into account the unnecessary depletion of resources, which includes clean water, good soil, and fuel needed to grow, store, and transport the foodstuffs—or the methane gas produced when thirty-five million tons of food rots in a land-fill. Or the collateral damage of throwing away food when one out of six Americans face hunger.[18]

Unless we personally experience the effects of global warming such as environmentally related illness, loss of housing, polluted land and water, or the disappearance of favorite creatures, the reality of our planet's suffering can be kept at an impervious distance. Life continues onward, and we forget that not many years ago none of us bought bottled water or had second thoughts about the quality of the food we eat. We didn't worry about whether disease could be controlled or if children and creatures being birthed today would have the gift of breathing clean air in the future.

This same unawareness extends to that of nonhumans and the increase of their demise. If I ever had any doubt that creatures experience suffering, that doubt fled with Ajahn Brahm's account of a "giant and fearsome Irishman," a violent offender in an Australian prison. This man's job entailed shooting cows as part of a work program in the prison's slaughterhouse. He had no problem stunning and killing animals, until one day a cow came into the stainless-steel funnel where the animals stood as they were being shot. On that particular day, this cow walked in slowly, "lifted her head and stared at her executioner, absolutely still. The Irishman was so overcome, he couldn't lift his gun; nor could he take his eyes away from the eyes of the cow. He couldn't tell how long it took, but as the cow held him in eye contact, he noticed something that shook him even more." The cow began to cry; first the tears came from the left eye, and then the right. The water trickled down her face. The man could not bear what he was seeing. He fell down on his knees, and vowed never to kill anything again.[19]

It does not take a gun in one's hand to destroy creation. Humans do so by the unreflective way they live and the reckless use of Earth's resources. When I consider the impact of my daily life on our planet's failing health—what I eat, the clothes I wear, how I travel, how much "stuff" I have and never use, where my garbage goes—I realize how significantly I add to the cause of such ravage. The pesticides used on plants that grow my food become toxic for songbirds coming in contact with them. The meat I eat arrives from unregulated farm factories whose animal manure spills out into streams, killing fish and other wildlife. The fossil fuels that power my car add to the carbon pollution in the air. Everything I consume bears the mark of Earth's generosity.

In *Laudato Si'*, Pope Francis refers to his namesake, St. Francis of Assisi, to emphasize how we can extend our compassion:

> For to him each and every creature was a sister united to him by bonds of affection. That is why he felt called to care for all that exists. . . . Such a conviction

cannot be written off as naïve romanticism, for it affects the choices which determine our behavior. If we approach nature and the environment without this openness of awe and wonder, if we no longer speak the language of fraternity and beauty in our relationship to the world, our attitude will be that of masters, consumers, ruthless exploiters, unable to set limits on their immediate needs. By contrast, if we feel intimately united with all that exists, then sobriety and care will well up spontaneously.[20]

We have a choice. How will we choose to live?

REFLECTION

Visualize your favorite flower, food, and animal. How would you feel if any of these no longer existed? What if the special place in nature that you enjoy was destroyed?

PRAYER

Comforter of the Afflicted, I join my heart with yours today in mourning the loss of species that die long before their time.

SCRIPTURE TO CARRY IN YOUR HEART TODAY

"We know that the whole of creation has been groaning in labor pains until now" (Rom 8:22).

WEEK 5, DAY 4

NATURE AS "THOU"

The world about us has become
an "it" rather than a "thou."
—Thomas Berry, *The Great Work*[21]

On my way out of the Des Moines Art Center, my eyes caught a movement to my left. I saw a mother chipmunk trying to teach her youngster to climb up a four-foot concrete wall. The mother scampered up to the top of the wall, chattering support to the child. The young one attempted to climb up but could only make it partway. The mother quickly came down and chattered some more to the little one. Up the wall she went again, calling to him from the top with what I assumed to be something like, "C'mon, c'mon. I know you can do it." This pattern of teaching and coaxing, of going down and trying to get up, went on for the ten minutes that I watched them.

I became captivated by the mother's patience, thinking of the similarity between humans and creatures. The scene could easily have been one of a parent teaching a child to ride a bike or learn to walk. During the brief time that I observed the chipmunks, I felt a relationship with them. The longer I stood there, the more deeply absorbed I became in their situation. I felt less an observer and more a cheerleader. I wanted that little chipmunk to make it to the top.

Compassion for creation does not develop from being a bystander. Pierre Teilhard de Chardin, Jesuit priest and paleontologist, urged our coming close to creation: "To understand the world is not enough, you must see it, touch it, live in its presence and drink the vital heat of existence in the very heart of reality."[22]

We must find ways to be closely in touch with the natural world around us. When we do so, we experience this life as a "thou" rather than an "it."

In *The Great Work*, Thomas Berry laments the distance that has come between nature and humanity. Societal and cultural changes have led humans into a mode of thinking of creation as "a collection of objects rather than a communion of subjects. . . . We no longer hear the voice of the rivers, the mountains, or the sea. The trees and the meadows are no longer intimate modes of spirit presence."[23] Because of the increasing distance separating us, we stand apart and lose an awareness of what is happening to creation. Consequently, the damage done to nature fails to affect our minds and hearts.

Newsweek magazine published an article written by John Luma, showing how effective "coming close" to nature can be in transforming our relationship with this part of life. Luma moved from a cool, objective view to one in which he experienced a sense of communion. This came about when he responded to a request from his wife while he was working in his home office. She noticed some baby mockingbirds had fallen out of their nest and wondered if John could go outside and help them. He did so reluctantly, not having much interest in outdoor life and hesitant to leave his work. Once he picked up the fragile birds, however, his attitude began to change. Only one bird had survived the fall. John fed and cared for this survivor during the next two weeks. He kept it safe at night in a nested box in the guest bathroom, got up from his sleep for regular feedings, and carefully guarded the bird as it learned to fly. At the end of the article, Luma marveled: "Our bond deepened into something totally unexpected. I became one with that bird, with nature."[24]

John Luma deliberately gave himself to a situation that brought him into a "thou" relationship. Sometimes this experience is reversed. It is nature that reaches out to us. For example, the seventeenth-century Carmelite monk Br. Lawrence was simply standing before a winter tree when he felt his heart enkindled with love for the Holy One as he pondered the tree's seasonal process. This sense of divine love stayed with Br. Lawrence for the rest of his life.[25] Similarly, Macrina Wiederkehr tells of a morning during her teenage years when "the spectacular colors of the sunrise, and the dewy freshness of the morning worked an incredible healing in my life."[26]

Creation continually offers us opportunities to enter into a "thou" relationship if we are attentive and willing to be present. We can't force nature to inspire or teach us, but if we enter that realm with respectful attention and humble receptivity, we will eventually meet a "thou." Theologian Sally McFague offers encouragement in this regard: "One does not need mountains and rainforests—any body will do, if we are willing to pay attention to it as Meister Eckhart eloquently says: 'If I spent enough time with the tiniest creature—even a caterpillar—I would never have to prepare a sermon. So full of God is every creature.'"[27]

Spending time is the key, plus getting ourselves out of the picture long enough to become aware of the life of the other. You can do this by walking through the produce or florist section of a supermarket. Walk not as a consumer but as a wonder-seeker. Pause to behold the colors, shapes, textures, and scents of our generative planet. Stand by a tree, touch the bark, and think of how the roots, at that very moment, are sending nutrients up through the bark and into the branches and leaves. When you see a butterfly, pause and imagine how its beauty formed in the dark gestation of the chrysalis. Don't just step on grass; reach down and touch it. Taste the juice of an orange, and enter the journey of growth that orange took to become so delicious. When you care for your pets, join their world and leave your own behind for a while.

The sacredness of life, the *thou-ness*, is everywhere—if we but pause to observe and enter that domain.

REFLECTION

"Love all creation, the whole and every grain of it. . . . If you love everything, you will perceive the Divine Mystery in all things. . . . And once you perceive it, you will begin to comprehend better every day and shall come to love the whole world with an all-embracing love" (Fyodor Dostoyevsky).

Reflect on times when you entered into a "thou" relationship with nature.

PRAYER

"I pray that we . . . may grow in our understanding of the nature of all living beings and our connectedness with the natural world" (Jane Goodall).[28]

SCRIPTURE TO CARRY IN YOUR HEART TODAY

"Let the heavens be glad, and let the earth rejoice;

let the sea roar, and all that fills it;

let the field exult, and everything in it.

Then shall all the trees of the forest sing for joy." (Ps 96:11–12)

WEEK 5, DAY 5

THINKING LIKE A MOUNTAIN

When you really look at something
it becomes a part of you.

—John O'Donohue, *Anam Cara*[29]

The authors of *Thinking like a Mountain* encourage us to enter into the world of creation in a way that allows us to have an empathic sense of what nature experiences.[30] If we do this, our consciousness of the suffering inflicted on nature grows wider and clearer. On retreat days when I invite participants to reflect on compassion for creation, I encourage them to go outside and commune with a tree, a blade of grass, a bird, an insect, a stone—anything that draws their attention. I ask them to be with that species of nature and listen to its story, to imagine what it might be like to live in that particular form.

This exercise rests on the hope that the participants will recognize both the beauty and the vulnerability of what they're observing. Invariably, when they return indoors to talk about the process, most will have been unable to do this, keeping the focus on their human self instead. They offer anthropomorphic responses, comparing nature's story to their own: "My life has felt like that tree with its tattered leaves"; "I looked at the bird and remembered how I've gained greater freedom"; or "I don't want my heart to be as hard as this stone"; and so forth.

I invite you now to participate in this exercise, only you will not be stepping outdoors. You will be stepping into your mind to visualize each of the following scenarios. Do not hurry the reflection. Read each one, and pause to enter into the life of that particular situation before moving on to the next. Really "look" at each part of nature, as John O'Donohue indicates. Let it "become a part of you." Try to attain an empathic sense of the suffering inherent in the situation.

You are *a tree in a thickly wooded Brazilian rainforest*. You have always considered this your home and thought you had many more years of life in this green paradise. But now you hear the sound of angry pulsing motors. You see your relatives around you being felled by these machines. They are helpless against the enormous blades. Your leaves exhale once more to give oxygen for the benefit of creatures. Then you wait for the blow that will take your life, too.

You are *a river in a large city*. The freedom to flow and move unimpeded has never ceased to thrill you. Today as you pass a multibuilding factory, large globs of gray matter enter and thicken your waters. The fish that swim beneath your surface find it difficult to breathe. The gray matter keeps traveling with you no matter how fast you move. It hangs on to you tenaciously. You begin to feel as though you are slowly being strangled.

You are *a young albatross who has recently learned to fly*. How exciting to be on your own. But for several weeks now, you have not felt well. The things you have eaten leave something hard and stabbing in your stomach. Each day you feel greater weakness and wonder if you will have enough energy to fly and search for food. Your mother comes to be with you. She has tears in her eyes as she tells you she cannot take out the pieces of plastic lodged in your stomach.

You are *a colorful mountain*. Wildflowers spread across your meadows. Transparent creeks sing with joy. Pine trees stand tall and proud upon your hills. Birds of many kinds sing endlessly from morning to night. Peace fills the air. But now trucks and heavy equipment come charging in. The drivers speak of plans to strip your landscape of everything, including soil that has been there for centuries. Big teeth soon begin digging inside of you and gut out your minerals. When they have taken them all, they depart, leaving you naked and infertile.

You are *a baby elephant wandering in the savanna*. You hurried away with your parents when they were chased by poachers. The three of you ran and ran until exhausted as the gunshots rang out. Both of your parents were mercilessly murdered by the hunters, who sawed off their tusks to sell for ivory. You cry for your mother and do not know how you will survive without her, for she was still feeding you with her milk.

You are *one of the last specimens of the western prairie fringed orchid*. Your head sinks against your stem as you remember how it used to be. It seems only yesterday that all your aunts and uncles, cousins and siblings, danced in the breeze. Now you are one of the few left. You have grown thin and desperately ill. No amount of sunshine or rain gives you what you need. You are not sure if it's something in the soil or in the air, but you have a strong feeling that you too will soon be gone forever.

You are an *expansive ocean teeming with marine life*. Each year more plastics, garbage, and waste are thrown into your waters. You are the lifeblood of this planet's ecosystem. The more clogged you become with invasive trash from humans, the fewer creatures that survive or grow in you. You ask yourself: "Don't humans know three-fourths of their oxygen comes from oceans like myself? Why can't people stop shoving into me things that kill the life dwelling in my waters?"

REFLECTION

Write a letter to one of the endangered species in the above scenarios of suffering.

PRAYER

Nurturer of Life, draw me into the heart of creation. Nudge me often to experience both the joy and the sorrow that exist there. I desire to love creation in the way that you do.

SCRIPTURE TO CARRY IN YOUR HEART TODAY

"Consider the ravens: they neither sow nor reap, they have neither storehouse nor barn, and yet God feeds them" (Lk 12:24).

WEEK 5, DAY 6

CARING FOR EARTH

*Through everyday actions on everyday issues, we
are creating living economies, living democracies,
and living cultures. Diversity, alliances,
cooperation, and persistence are our strengths.
Service, support, and solidarity are our means.*

—Vandana Shiva, *Earth Democracy*[31]

Caring for Earth takes courage and requires conviction. Some environmentalists are scorned and demeaned with terms like "tree hugger," and their efforts to protect creation are considered to be that of worthless romantics. No one knew this dismissive rejection better than marine biologist Rachel Carson. Her scientific interest gradually turned to research that awakened the world about the destructive nature of DDT and other pesticides. More than fifty years ago when Carson's landmark book *Silent Spring* was published, antienvironmentalists and scoffers branded her a "peacenik" and communist. The FBI even went so far as to investigate her. Lobbyists for chemical industries tried to get her research dismissed as incompetent, and three key advertising sponsors dropped out of a planned television interview in an attempt to silence her ideas.[32]

In spite of this vociferous attack against Rachel Carson's work, within ten years after *Silent Spring* debuted, the Environmental Protection Agency was established and Earth Day started being celebrated as a way to encourage attention to environmental concerns. Our task to care for Earth these many years later ought to be much easier than Carson's because of an abundance of information about environmental issues and the continuous effort of ecologists to halt the rapid decline of our planet's health. Yet such is not the case. The challenges remain daunting. Enthusiasm and energy can be stifled by loud voices in denial about Earth's situation and by our own temptation to discount our endeavors to prevent harmful environmental situations. We dare not give in to that doubt, nor despair of the possibility of change.

During an interview, Jane Goodall was asked, "What do you see as the most important thing individuals can do to affect positive change for the environment?" Her answer is one that affirms each person who cares for Earth: "The most important thing we can do is remember that every single day one of us makes a difference. And we can all choose the kind of difference we're going to make." Goodall then gave an example of this: "Becoming aware about what we buy. Where does it come from? How was it grown? Did it involve the use of child labor or chemical pesticides? The big problem today is that so many people feel insignificant."[33]

Turning toward mentors of environmental change can help inspire and encourage our attempts to care for Earth, no matter how small those efforts might seem. I consider Vandana Shiva to

be one of these mentors. I first became acquainted with this In-
dian physicist's dedicated environmental work when I viewed
a forum of the Johannesburg World Summit on Sustainable Development. I asked myself, "Who is this knowledgeable woman
who speaks passionately about tending to the needs of our planet and helping the most vulnerable people?"

Vandana Shiva understands the dynamics and hidden agendas behind the posturing of large corporations claiming to aid
impoverished people, but which actually focus on profits for their
companies. At the same time, she encourages people around the
globe to join cooperatively in caring for Earth. She does so with a
view similar to that of Jane Goodall—believing our daily efforts
are significant: "We are reclaiming a world precariously on the
edge. We take action not with arrogance and certainty, but with
humility and uncertainty. It is our giving that counts—not our
success. But in selfless giving, we have victories. And through
everyday actions, we reweave the web of life."[34]

Unless we have been living in a hole for years, we know
what those everyday actions might be. Among them: being careful about how much water we use, less purchasing of things we
do not need, reusing and recycling as many products as possible, avoiding use of plastics that pollute, traveling in ways that
lessen the carbon effects of fossil fuels, being attentive to deter-
gents and chemical products that add to toxic waste, purchasing
food grown locally, and living altogether more simply. If each
person in well-developed countries made an effort to live in this
manner every day, poverty across the globe would be greatly
reduced and Earth could breathe much easier.

But personal efforts alone will not stem the tide of environmental suffering and planetary harm. The health of Earth relies
heavily on political legislation to create controls and standards
regarding environmental issues on both global and regional lev-
els. Without this dimension of global care, the suffering of our

planet will continue to increase. In *Laudato Si'*, Pope Francis reminds us: "Our planet is a homeland and . . . humanity is one people living in a common home. . . . Everything is related, and we human beings are united as brothers and sisters on a wonderful pilgrimage, woven together by the love God has for each of [God's] creatures and which also unites us in fond affection with brother sun, sister moon, brother river and mother earth."[35]

The implications of this global relationship and interdependence prompt us to live in a manner benefiting the well-being of everyone and everything. This knowledge also leads us to promote and support justice for our planet through governmental regulation. We know that what we choose to do, or not do, will affect not just our personal life but the lives of all on our beloved Earth.

REFLECTION

"We can help heal this world and unify it in love, or we can destroy its inner unity by our resistance to evolve in love" (Ilia Delio, *The Emergent Christ*).[36]

What is one deliberate action you will take to assist in maintaining the health of and healing the wounds of our planet?

PRAYER

"May we who dream of peace awaken anew to the Spirit of God who calls us to pursue our dreams in concrete ways. May God continue to bless us with wisdom, with wellsprings of rest, and with passion for our paths. And one day we may gather with all creation at the place where the mountains dance and the river flows with peace, with justice, and with delight in all our sacred journeys" (Jan Richardson, *Sacred Journeys*).[37]

SCRIPTURE TO CARRY IN YOUR HEART TODAY

"How very good and pleasant it is

when kindred live together in unity!" (Ps 133:1)

WEEK 5, DAY 7

REVIEW AND REST

> *The concrete tangibility of the earth, the fragility of*
> *the living world, the haunting beauty of nature—all*
> *these [are] . . . potentially a means for divine disclosure.*
> *The human experience of the senses—of seeing, touching*
> *and feeling—could reveal a path leading to the "heart of*
> *reality," to God. [There is] a deeper unity of all things,*
> *with their diversity ultimately held together by God.*
> —Pierre Teilhard de Chardin[38]

Choose any or all of the following as a way to review Week Five:

- What three aspects of "A Thousand Unbreakable Links" were of greatest significance to you this past week?

- As you look over the week, did you notice any part of creation's suffering that you had not been aware of in the past? If so, how did that affect you?

- If you were to tell someone from another planet about Earth, how would you describe our planet?

- In what way might this week's study have led you to a keener sense of the interdependence of all that exists?

- Which day's reflection challenged you the most?

- Which one left you nodding your head yes?

- As you look back over your lived week, what particular moments or situations awakened you both to the beauty and the wounds of our planet?

- Take an hour to be with some form of nonhuman life: animals, plants, birds, and so on. Observe with your senses. Get to know what you are observing as a "thou." Keep your own interests and thoughts out of the way. Be present as a companion in a caring relationship.

- List the ways that you have observed the suffering of creation during the past week. Write a psalm of lament in Earth's voice.

$\mathcal{B}$ECOMING A COMPASSIONATE PRESENCE

INTRODUCTION

Every great dream begins with a dreamer. Always
remember, you have within you the strength, the patience,
and the passion to reach for the stars to change the world.

—Harriet Tubman[1]

In this last week, I send you forth to live more fully what you have learned and integrated into your understanding of compassion. These days provide both spiritual and scientific insights to encourage you to expand loving-kindness wherever you are. The topics are meant to buoy your motivation and hope, while also being realistic regarding the ongoing challenges of compassion. The ultimate question is this: Will you trust that your loving presence and good deeds contribute to the dream of peace and toward the diminishment of travail in our world?

Thomas Kelly, Quaker educator and scholar, writes of "a tendering of the soul toward everything in creation." This *tendering* comes about because the soul has been "enfolded in divine Love . . . which *embraces all creation.*" Kelly envisions this faithful Presence as "an infinite ocean of light and love which is flowing over the ocean of darkness and death."[2] With this radiant movement of divinity in our soul, we are strengthened to engage empathically with the sorrows and burdens of a troubled world.

On Day 5 of this week I suggest that you reflect on mentors of compassion. Their witness of nonjudgmental inclusivity, fierce determination, and willingness to pay the price for change serves as an inspiration and stimulus for hope. Dorothy Day, who worked tirelessly to welcome people lacking shelter and the basics of life, had no idea how widespread and effective her hard work would be. She simply focused her efforts on a desire to help "build a society where it's easier for people to be good to each other."[3] This desire involved more than idealistic theories or far-off goals. Dorothy worked tirelessly to promote this intention, including sharing in the household duties and exhausting details of providing shelter for homeless and disenfranchised persons in the Catholic Worker house.

Our compassionate actions do not have to be enormous projects. Daily acts of kindness, considerate understanding, and spontaneous generosity may not appear to have a great effect, and yet they have the power to ease the pain of negativity and cradle a buoyancy in another person's heart. For example, a friend of mine told me about writing a note of thanks to her family physician after he discovered a tumor that could have developed into a life-threatening cancer for her husband. To her surprise, the doctor sent a response. It read: "Your kind words brought tears to my eyes. I am so happy that I could have a positive impact on your health care. I try to give my best to every patient I see. Unfortunately, the majority of feedback I get is negative. Patient expectations are so high it becomes difficult to meet them. I keep the encouraging cards like yours to read again later. It has been more than a year since I received one."

Think of how that simple card eased the dose of negativity thrust on this physician, how it reenergized his intention to give compassionate care as best he could. We never know what one thoughtful act of kindness might engender in the life of another, or how far-reaching that deed might be.

Singer and songwriter Carrie Newcomer refers to this when commenting about her song "Help in Hard Times": "The things that have saved us, the things that have always saved us—as individuals and communities—are still here. Compassion, kindness, hospitality, generosity, and good parenting didn't go away because we are in a particular civil-political season right now. These are completely accessible within us and between us."[4] We surely need political, social, and church leaders who are willing to acknowledge and enter the suffering of humanity, leaders who will lay their lives on the line to bring about justice for those who are oppressed. But, as Newcomer reminds us, every person can contribute to being an agent of change.

When Jesus announced to his disciples, "You are the light of the world" (Mt 5:14), he was also speaking to every one of us. I wonder what tone of voice and which words Jesus emphasized when he made that statement. Given his kindly approach to others, I daresay his voice filled with an affectionate confidence, emphasizing *you* and *light*. If we could hear him speak to us today, he might reword that proclamation: "*You* are the *compassion* of the world."

WEEK 6, DAY 1

OUR COMMON HUMANITY

Love is a spiritual practice. It doesn't happen
automatically. We have to practice loving.

—Macrina Wiederkehr, *Abide*[5]

I used to believe the day would come when I developed compassion so thoroughly that I might respond automatically to suffering. I've learned that compassion takes practice. Like physical exercise, I must regularly recall the basic tenets and deliberately act on them if I intend to live this foundational virtue of Christianity.

Even now, I am surprised how I can still slip into a pattern of forgetfulness when activities and deadlines crowd my days— too much "me-ness" and not enough "oneness." This fosters an unawareness of how others are suffering. The reality of my oneness with the rest of life slips into the closet of forgetfulness, along with compassionate action. I can also go to the other extreme, as I did during the years when my good friend had lung cancer, and become so absorbed in another's suffering that my own life barely finds a resting place.

Yes, a healthy life of compassion requires practice, but it also needs balance. Thinking too much or too little about self, caring too much or too little about others—any of these throws compassion's effectiveness off balance and creates more suffering. In Week Two I referred to reflecting on "our common humanity" as a way to ease our personal suffering. Today we see how the recognition of our common humanity motivates us to reach beyond ourselves to the wider world, to establish a healthy balance in extending loving-kindness to others.

Native Americans have a long history of envisioning this connectedness. They consider it to be a natural consequence of all beings sharing life together, related to one another and to the universe. The Sioux people use the phrase *Mitakuye Oyasin*—"all my relatives"—to begin and end their prayers. Other tribes, such as the Cherokee, have a similar tradition. This practice supports a constant remembrance of our interdependence with one another.[6]

Harry Palmer designed a simple exercise to encourage empathy. He suggests we approach another with the intention of finding a commonality in our humanity. As we gaze upon this person, we remind ourselves that he or she is much like our self in wanting happiness and avoiding suffering, in knowing difficulties and seeking inner peace. When we understand this link of our humanity, it keeps us from being too self-oriented and strengthens our capacity to be compassionate to the other person.[7]

Another advantage of Palmer's exercise resides in its ability to widen our mind and heart by accepting those who differ significantly from us. The more we are in touch with our mutual basic tendencies and desires, the stronger our inclination toward kindhearted openness. In my youth, we Roman Catholics marginalized our Protestant neighbors because of required regulations by the Church. I was taught that my Catholic faith was the superior religion. Consequently, I rarely associated with Protestants until I entered college. There, I happily learned from personal friendships how much we had in common, and how much more alike we were than different.

In 2009, the Charter for Compassion was created by an international group of religious leaders. It includes a call to respect all religious traditions:

> We therefore call upon all men and women to restore compassion to the center of morality and religion—to return to the ancient principle that any interpretation of scripture that breeds violence, hatred or disdain is illegitimate—to ensure that youth are given accurate and respectful information about other traditions, religions and cultures—to encourage a positive appreciation of cultural and religious diversity—to cultivate an informed empathy with the suffering of all human beings—even those regarded as enemies.[8]

Religious differences continue to produce acute suffering when those disparities are not respected due to arrogance, fear, or ignorance. Palmer's exercise helps to alleviate hostility and disparagement of other religions when we remember, *Just like me, these persons also seek a life that gives them meaning. Just like me, these people search for how best to live.* This awareness serves to bond us in the similar hope of obtaining peace of mind and heart. Of course, we also experience a unity with persons of other religions and no religion in our shared experience of suffering. As

Gail Straub notes, "The gift of the awakened heart is that all suffering in some way belongs to all of us. Here we experience the mysterious intimacy that connects us to everything that lives."[9]

We are more alike than unalike, whether in regard to religion or any other difference that tends to divide us. The following quotation from the late Henri Nouwen calls for much pondering:

> Compassion grows with the inner recognition that your neighbor shares your humanity with you. This partnership cuts through all walls which might have kept you separate. Across all barriers of land and language, wealth and poverty, knowledge and ignorance, we are one, created from the same dust, subject to the same laws, destined for the same end. With this compassion you can say, "In the face of the oppressed I recognize my own face and in the hands of the oppressor I recognize my hands. Their flesh is my flesh; their blood is my blood; their pain is my pain; their smile is my smile. Their ability to torture is in me, too; their capacity to forgive I find also in myself. There is nothing in me that does not belong to them, too. There is nothing in them that does not belong to me, too. In my heart, I know their yearning for love and down to my entrails, I can feel their cruelty. In another's eyes, I see my plea for forgiveness and in a hardened frown, I see my refusal. . . . In the depths of my being, I meet my fellow humans with whom I share love and hate, life and death."[10]

So the next time someone rankles your mental or emotional equilibrium, please pause and gaze on them with as much openness as possible. Ask yourself: "In what way do the two of us share a similarity in our common humanity? How are we more alike than unalike?"

REFLECTION

"We should recognize our shared humanity. These are our human brothers and sisters, who have the same right and the same desire to have a happy life. . . . We are part of the same society. We are part of the same humanity. When humanity is happy, we will be happy. When humanity is peaceful, our own lives are peaceful" (Dalai Lama and Desmond Tutu, *The Book of Joy*).[11]

What does "our common humanity" mean to you in your practice of compassion?

PRAYER

"How great are the needs of Your creatures on this earth, O God. I embark on a slow voyage of exploration with everyone who comes to me. Sometimes they seem to me like houses with open doors. I walk in and roam through passages and rooms, and every house is furnished a little differently, and yet they are all of them the same, and every one must be turned into a dwelling dedicated to You, oh God" (Etty Hillesum, *An Interrupted Life*).[12]

SCRIPTURE TO CARRY IN YOUR HEART TODAY

"Abide in me as I abide in you" (Jn 15:4).

WEEK 6, DAY 2

HOW SCIENCE BENEFITS COMPASSION

All our actions in the world are creating
fields of energy that will either be of great
assistance or will leave a harmful legacy.

—Paula D'Arcy, *Stars at Night*[13]

One winter I led a six-week retreat on compassion every Tuesday evening. Our group of adults met in an elementary school's multipurpose room. In the hallway a large wall banner displayed this message: "Watch your thoughts, they become words. Watch your words, they become actions. Watch your actions, they become habits. Watch your habits, they become character. Watch your character, it becomes destiny." I stood there quite amazed and thought, "That summarizes this evening's presentation."

Science, as noted in Week One, accompanies spirituality as a valuable instrument. The wall banner named succinctly how our brains are fundamentally involved in activating compassion. Knowledge gained from neuroscience assures us that we can use our brain in "watching" our judgments before choosing our behavior. Quantum physics also assists us in practicing compassion by assuring us of our intricate relationship with all that exists. This invisible bond encourages us to treat both human and nonhuman life with kindness, doing to others as we wish them to do to us (see Mt 7:12).

Judy Cannato explores another effective way that science enables us to live more compassionately. In *Field of Compassion*, she bases her insights on biologist Rupert Sheldrake's theory of morphogenic fields. To *morph* means to undergo a gradual transformation.

Sheldrake taught that all living forms have a field or region of energy within and around them that carries information, habits, and memories that contribute to change. Cannato explains: "Each person is a morphogenic field, as is each group we belong to. There are morphogenic fields of atoms, cells, molecules, rabbits, elephants, petunias, etc." Sheldrake believed that new behavior patterns develop due to the strength and influence of the energy field.[14]

These electromagnetic fields can be compared to the invisible power of magnets to attract or repel. Cannato explains that this field of energy grows and establishes itself with repeated patterns of thought and behavior. She illustrates this theory with Sheldrake's scientific cases to show how a repeated action eventually builds up a strong energy field. The following case especially intrigued me.

In the early 1920s, milk in glass bottles was delivered to the doorsteps of households in England. Small birds learned how to tear the cardboard tops off the milk bottles and sip the cream. Bird-watchers who traced this behavior noticed that this same species of bird hundreds of miles away began doing the same thing. This surprised scientists because these particular birds rarely flew more than fifteen miles from their habitat. So how did they learn this? The morphogenic field of information (how to tear off the cardboard tops) became strong enough to influence the behavior of birds farther away. When World War II arrived, the milk bottle delivery stopped. It did not resume until about five years longer than the life span of these birds. Yet within months of milk being delivered to doorsteps, this same species of bird began lifting off the tops and drinking the cream. Within a year or two similar birds were doing this as far away as Holland. The morphogenic field held the memory of this learned behavior so that birds born later had access to its information.[15]

So what does this have to do with compassion? Cannato tells us: "There is no insignificant thought, word, or action. Each act of courage and strength shifts the energy and increases the potential for others to become aware, too. No matter what we do, we are always affecting the energy around us, in either a negative or a positive way." She then suggests that Jesus created a morphogenic field "in which love was the standard operating procedure."[16] The more we practice being compassionate, the stronger this morphogenic field develops. For example, if we continually strive to end negative or prejudicial thoughts about others, we can build up an ability to cease these thoughts. As this morphogenic field continues to strengthen, it enables others to lessen their negative thoughts as well.

Along with Sheldrake's theory of morphogenic fields, there is yet another concept that can benefit our compassionate behavior. A clerk at our local post office presented a perpetually disgruntled expression, one that led me to think he either hated his job or had some type of emotional disorder. I never saw him smile, ever. Anytime I went to the post office, I would leave feeling grouchy. Then one day I read about "mirror neurons" and found a positive way to counteract my negative response. Christopher Germer describes how mirror neurons act in *The Mindful Path to Self-Compassion*:

> The building blocks for empathizing with other people are the "mirror neurons," located primarily in the insula . . . and premotor strip . . . of the brain. Mirror neurons mimic motor neurons—the ones that control our muscles. The way empathy seems to occur is that when you see another person's face, the mirror neurons will mimic what you see so you can feel what the other person is feeling. For example, if you see a person smile, the mirror neurons will make your face

muscles smile and then you will feel yourself smiling and recognize what the other person is feeling. . . .

Our mirror neurons start firing as soon as we focus on another person. Happy or unhappy, friend or foe? We can often detect tiny changes in facial expression or verbal tone that reveal how another person is feeling, even though we're not fully aware of it.[17]

So when I see someone whose facial expression exhibits a certain emotion, my brain is registering that same emotion as if it is mine. Had I been aware of this, I could have chosen to smile instead of feeling irritated about the postal clerk's demeanor. Every positive thought, word, and deed contributes to strengthening compassion. Every facial expression, too, holds the possibility of lessening suffering.

REFLECTION

How are you contributing to the strength of a morphogenic field of compassion by your repeated patterns of thought and action?

PRAYER

Compassionate One, may my face show kindness. May my thoughts reinforce acceptance of differences. May my heart send forth love to strengthen the field of compassion.

SCRIPTURE TO CARRY IN YOUR HEART TODAY

"In everything do to others as you would have them do to you" (Mt 7:12).

WEEK 6, DAY 3

PAYING THE PRICE

Martin Luther King Jr. died daily, as St. Paul said.
He faced death daily and said a number of times
that he knew he would be killed for the faith
that was in him. . . . The faith that man is capable
of change, of growth, of growing in love.
—Dorothy Day, *Dorothy Day: Selected Writings*[18]

A longtime friend and I hiked in the Rocky Mountains one summer. In our midsixties, we felt invigorated the morning we departed for the seven-mile climb up to three pristine glacial lakes. After a mile or so on the trail, we halted abruptly in front of a low-lying creek with two feet of wildly rushing water covering the flooded path. As we looked on disappointedly, I wailed, "We'll have to turn back. It's too dangerous to cross." Instead of agreeing, Mary Kay suggested, "Let's see if there's another place." So we trekked alongside in the tangled brush until we came to a fallen tree trunk lying across the creek. "Let's cross on that log," she said. I looked at her in utter amazement, fear taking hold of me from my feet to my forehead. "You've got to be kidding," I protested. "Yes," she insisted, "we can toss our daypacks over to the other side before we cross over." And away she went like a gazelle in a field, safely to the other side. Me? I crawled trembling on my hands and knees, clinging to the log like a bat on the ceiling of a cave. But I too made it to the other side.

Crossing over a log on a rushing stream hardly compares to the enormous price people pay for their compassion, and yet it serves as a metaphor for those brave men and women who find themselves at seemingly impassable streams of suffering. They do not give up but choose, instead, to find a way to meet that suffering even when it means extreme hardship and the possibility of death.

The costs of compassion are many and varied, but they have one thing in common: a price to be paid. Sometimes this can be anticipated, but most often one does not fully know the cost until having set foot on the path. This cost might entail precious time and energy; poor health from overextension; bruised relationships or damaged reputation due to a stance for justice; feelings of vulnerability, discomfort, or uncertainty; leaving the safety and security of home; loss of a job; or the giving of one's physical life.

Risk-taking, courage that overcomes fear, and a firm belief in the value and necessity of a compassionate presence provide an impetus for many who give generously of their compassion. Missionaries do this routinely. Departing for countries engulfed with political unrest and societal injustice, they know their lives are in danger. Sr. Dorothy Stang, S.N.D., knew this when she ministered in Brazil. She was murdered in the Amazon basin because of her unwavering defense of subsistence farmers whose land was exploited and stolen by rich loggers and cattle ranchers.[19]

When we turn the pages of history, countless stories appear of men and women whose belief in justice gave them the brave determination to help change the future for those suffering from discrimination or disregard. The 2016 film *Loving* reveals the true story of the price extracted from an interracial couple choosing marriage at a time when Alabama law still prohibited it. They endured intimidation by police and degrading remarks of townspeople; and they were forced by court decision to live out of state away from family connections, and under penalty of prison if they returned to visit. After years of duress, with the help of a compassionate lawyer, they went to court and finally won, a decision that significantly impacted the future for other interracial marriages.

The investigative team of journalists at the *Boston Globe* who exposed the pedophile priest scandal in the Boston archdiocese experienced a different kind of cost. Theirs consisted of long, draining hours working to uncover the facts. Maintaining their courage was equally difficult as they took on the daunting task of confronting a strong Catholic establishment in order to disclose the truth. Their investigation eventually led to sexual abuse victims coming forward, a movement that opened the door to justice and the prospect of healing.

Franz Jägerstätter, an Austrian farmer and devout Catholic, gave his life rather than add to the suffering inflicted by Hitler's regime. Franz was beheaded for refusing to serve in the Nazi army. His neighbors considered him a religious fanatic. His pastor and bishop tried to discourage him. The one person who stood by his side was his wife, Franziska. She honored his conscience and supported his decision, even though they had three young daughters.

Gregory Boyle, S.J., termed "the Gandhi of gangs," dedicates his life to working with gangs in Los Angeles. As the founder of Homeboy Industries, he pours his compassion out in tireless efforts to help gang members choose another way to live. His investment in their lives also carries the ongoing sorrow of their deaths. In twelve years' time, he officiated at 167 funerals of these young people he has come to know and love—such a heavy price for a compassionate heart to bear.[20]

During the time that the Dakota Oil Access Pipeline was being challenged, the media reported on the astounding decisions that protesters made in order to stand strong in their hope of protecting the land. One man sold his home. A woman quit her job. Others put their belongings in storage and left behind families to be there for an unknown length of time. The activists gave up their comforts of home, experienced wild snowstorms, and accepted winter hardships while living in tents.[21]

Jesus paid the price for his desire to create a world of loving-kindness. His death came about because his teachings and actions challenged religious and political establishments. He spoke of peace, not war; of forgiveness, not vengeance; of kindness, not judgment; of mercy, not condemnation; of love, not fear.

I ask myself: "Am I willing to pay the price for the compassion I desire for people near or far away? Do I desire it enough to accept what my choices may cost me when I give from what is truest in my heart?"

REFLECTION

"To be utterly dependent on other people. To be ignored and despised and forgotten. To know little of respectability or comfort. To take orders and work hard for little or no money; it is a hard school, and one which most pious people do their best to avoid" (Thomas Merton, *New Seeds of Contemplation*).[22]

What do you most fear in "paying the price" for being compassionate?

PRAYER

Giver of All Good Gifts, open my mind to see how best to share my talents and treasures. Open my heart to release fear of paying the price for compassionate presence. Open my hands both to give and to receive in a way that reflects your love.

SCRIPTURE TO CARRY IN YOUR HEART TODAY

"If any want to become my followers, let them deny themselves and take up their cross and follow me" (Mk 8:34).

WEEK 6, DAY 4

ONE GOOD DEED

The things that matter most in our lives are not fantastic or grand. They are the moments when we touch one another, when we are there in the most attentive and caring way.

—Jack Kornfield, *A Path with Heart*[23]

In *A Path with Heart*, Jack Kornfield describes how he asked participants to imagine they were near death. He then invited them to look back over their lives to remember two good deeds of theirs. None of the actions they remembered were grandiose. Participants told of simple, touching moments like telling a father, "I love you," before he dies, or leaving a busy life to fly across the country and care for a sister's children while she heals from a car accident. An elementary school teacher recalled her good deeds as "the mornings when she held the children who were crying and having a hard day."[24]

Never discount a simple gesture of compassion. One good deed can impact a lifetime. Each touch of kindness can make a difference. Turning points of major import have taken place because one person reached out to another, or arrived with kindness at just the right moment. The phrase "one person at a time" indicates the necessity and efficacy of individual, compassionate actions. I became more convinced of this when I read the story of Deo Gratias, a medical student in Burundi, and noticed how one compassionate deed led to another—and how these individual kindnesses saved his life.

During the civil war and genocide in Burundi, Deo Gratias was working as an intern in a rural hospital when Hutu militiamen attacked the building and burned alive the Tutsi staff and patients. Deo Gratias, a Tutsi himself, managed to escape and ran with terror for weeks to avoid the marauding militia. He struggled through country brush and dangerous territories, passing horrific scenes, including mutilated dead bodies being devoured by dogs. He had little food and only dirty water. Finally, completely exhausted and ill, Deo Gratias could go no further. He was ready to die when an older Hutu woman stopped and urged him to his feet. She risked her life to help Deo to reach the Rwandan border, where he entered a refugee camp. He moved from one miserable camp to another for six months, until a medical student's father gave him $200 and a ticket to New York. Deo landed in the big city homeless, friendless, and jobless. He slept in abandoned buildings and ate from dumpsters for months until finding part-time work delivering groceries.

Then, a third compassionate person entered Deo's life. When the housekeeper at a Catholic rectory where he made a delivery saw how emaciated Deo looked, she took him under her wing after he shared his story. She managed to find housing for Deo in a small apartment with two Yale University professors. With the assistance of these two (yet two more people who reached out with good deeds), Deo reentered medical school, this time at Yale.[25]

Good deeds take place amid everyday lives. It does not take much for selfless, thoughtful consideration to influence others in a positive way. English author Margaret Silf confirms this in an article about the experience of drivers using a toll road for their travel to work. A commuter told her that every morning he noticed five toll booths with short lines, and a sixth one with a long line. He wondered about this and learned that the long line was due to the person working in that particular toll booth. This worker took a personal interest in each driver that passed by. Without fail, he greeted everyone warmly, asking how they and their families were doing. One recipient of this kindness was a driver who had lost his glasses. The compassionate toll-booth worker noticed this and expressed concern. Even the driver's own family had not been aware of the loss.

Silf concludes: "Such was the power of this 'one' that harassed drivers would line up, adding five or ten minutes to their commute, simply to be refreshed by this man's friendly words and authentic kindness. It is easy, it appears, for just one person to bring springs of new life into a world that routine stress has rendered so toxic. . . . Just one person can bring springs of new life into a stress-filled world."[26]

Just as one person can ease the pain of another, so too can one person impact the larger community. Every organization or social movement for good begins with one caring individual whose vision and passion ignite the light in other hearts. Together they gain strength in eliminating the aches of our world. Social worker Leymah Gbowee, for example, organized the Women of Liberia Mass Action for Peace when she could no longer endure the killings and lack of safety for the Liberian people, especially their children. She began by praying and singing in a fish market. From there she invited Christian and Muslim women to come together to pray for peace and join in nonviolent protest.

This movement of women dressed in white grew until it numbered in the thousands. They became a strong voice objecting to the country's violence and governmental corruption. Day after day, week after week, they sat steadfastly in front of President Charles Taylor's residence. They endured steamy African sun and heavy rains, persisting in their request that he meet with the rebels and negotiate a peace settlement. No amount of discomfort or discouragement stopped the women from protesting daily. With Leymah Gbowee's leadership, they finally forced the stalled peace talks to resume between Taylor and the rebels. The two sides negotiated a settlement, and peace was restored in Liberia, due in large part to this one woman's "good deed" and to the others who joined with their "one good deed" in that government-changing action.

"One person at a time." Remember this when you are tempted to think your one small gesture of compassion won't make a difference.

REFLECTION

"Whatever our part is, just do one thing. That's all we have to do. The guilt—or the curse—of the progressive, the liberal, the whatever, is that we think we have to do it all. And then we get overwhelmed. . . . Community is about just doing my part" (Sr. Simone Campbell, as quoted in Krista Tippett's *Becoming Wise*).[27]

Look back on your life. Find one good deed of yours that made a difference.

PRAYER

Companion of Every Soul, I am but one person in a world saturated with suffering. Help me to avoid the desire to see results. I will trust that each gesture of kindness, each desire to care, and each decision to love has value. I will do my part.

SCRIPTURE TO CARRY IN YOUR HEART TODAY

"If a brother or sister is naked and lacks daily food, and one of you says to them, 'Go in peace; keep warm and have your fill,' and yet you do not supply their bodily needs, what is the good of that?" (Jas 2:15–16).

WEEK 6, DAY 5

MENTORS OF COMPASSION

If we see only the worst, it destroys our capacity to do something. If we remember those times and places—and there are so many—where people have behaved magnificently, this gives us energy to act, and at least the possibility of sending this spinning top of the world in a different direction.

—Howard Zinn, "The Optimism of Uncertainty"[28]

The circle of compassion grows larger when we look around and notice people who "have behaved magnificently" when facing suffering. Their greatness of heart evokes inspiration, courage, and determination. While every person bears qualities of compassion, people become mentors by the way they activate these virtues. I mention just a few of them here. These people are public figures. Many mentors of compassion are not. They live in our neighborhoods, church communities, among our relatives and friends. No one sets out to be a teacher of compassion. This happens through the way one responds to suffering in its many forms.

Kinship with Disenfranchised People: Dorothy Day, cofounder of the Catholic Worker movement, motivates this quality in my heart. I value Dorothy's compassion because she was honest about how difficult this relationship with impoverished people can sometimes be. She had faults, and she knew failure. There was nothing romantic about how Dorothy engaged in the tumbling ups and downs of this kinship. Dorothy's love of people who struggle with life's inequities gave her the incentive to stay in the fray—along with her continual yearning for a faith strong enough to see her through difficult situations.

A Willingness to Be Vulnerable: Nelson Mandela has been lauded for many of his valuable virtues, all of which led him to be an inspiring and compassionate president of South Africa. What stands out for me is how he turned from being an angry, vengeful dissident to a man with a wide heart, opening himself to others in a kindhearted, defenseless posture. Mandela moved from his place on the pedestal of rebel leadership to become a common prisoner among other prisoners. His kindness and lack of arrogance welcomed those around him as other human beings on the path of life. No wonder he was deeply respected by them.

The Strength of Divine Indwelling: I return frequently to Etty Hillesum's diaries and letters. When Etty discloses the intimate relationship she has with the Holy One in *An Interrupted Life,* she helps me believe in my own energy for good that comes from an indwelling, compassionate Presence. This Jewish woman, who died in Auschwitz at age twenty-nine, exudes a depth of compassion and emotional strength that parallels her ever-growing relationship with the Holy One. Etty felt the pain of a society filled with animosity and degradation but refused to hate in return. She suffered deprivation and personal illness, lost loved ones to the Gestapo before she herself was taken, and yet she returned time and again to a compassionate response. In one of her prayers, Etty writes, "I shall try to follow wherever Your hand leads me and shall try to not be afraid. I shall try to spread some of my warmth, of my genuine love for others, wherever I go."[29]

Patient Fortitude: Mother Teresa of Calcutta believed strongly in her vision for good. While being renowned for her charitable work with the destitute and dying, she is less well known for her endurance in requesting permission from the Church hierarchy to found the Missionaries of Charity. When Mother Teresa applied to establish this community, she followed Church protocol without complaint. This process consisted of years of endless red tape, jumping through the hoops of answering questions and providing details, waiting for long periods before responses arrived, then having to answer more concerns, always with the intent of having to prove her capability for leading a community of sisters. Mother Teresa persisted in her request because she trusted in her vision of ministry to love and serve the forgotten ones of Calcutta's streets and slums. This allowed her to tolerate long years of waiting.

Fierce Compassion: I first came across this term in China Galland's book *The Bond between Women: A Journey to Fierce Compassion*. Galland writes from her experience of interviewing women across the globe. The more she uncovered stories of women and children suffering from cultural injustice and disparity, the more she believed in anger as a viable response. Galland explains, "Compassionate rage does not kill anything or anyone. It does not harm. It is different from anger without compassion. Anger without compassion wants to kill the 'other.'" But compassionate wrath, or creative resistance, means being willing to put oneself on the line—to put your own body in front of the trees, not to point a gun at someone else. "Creative resistance is not against a person but against a system."[30] Groups such as Mothers of the Disappeared in Argentina let their anger and sorrow be heard as they cried out in protest against the loss of their abducted children who "disappeared" during the terrorism that raged in their country. They are inspiration for everyone whose anger at appalling injustice leads to a strong protest.

Experience of Intense Suffering: Some of the most compassionate people I've known have suffered greatly. They took what they experienced and used the wisdom of their experience to seed it into a life of loving-kindness. Martin Luther King Jr., Mahatma

Gandhi, Aung San Suu Kyi, John Lewis, and Thich Nhat Hanh are among my mentors who allowed their suffering to be transformed into the gold of compassion. These mentors remind me of what Swiss psychiatrist Elizabeth Kübler-Ross uncovered in her research on death and dying: "The most beautiful people we have known are those who have known defeat, known suffering, known struggle, known loss, and have found their way out of the depths. These persons have an appreciation, a sensitivity, and an understanding of life that fills them with compassion, gentleness, and a deep loving concern. Beautiful people do not just happen."[31]

Whoever our mentors might be, whether a Mahatma Gandhi teaching by his life that injustice can be overcome with a nonviolent approach, or a Mother Teresa of Calcutta witnessing by her work among people in destitution that each kind gesture is the gesture of Christ, let us be mindful that those who mentor us in compassion do not just happen. They are mentors because they believed in and followed the love in their hearts.

REFLECTION

Who are your mentors of compassion? How have they inspired you?

PRAYER

Thank you, Vessel of Divine Love, for the witness of men and women of compassion. May their lives kindle a spark in my heart that impassions me to share your love to the fullest.

SCRIPTURE TO CARRY IN YOUR HEART TODAY

"Now in Joppa there was a disciple whose name was Tabitha, which in Greek is Dorcas. She was devoted to good works and acts of charity" (Acts 9:36).

WEEK 6, DAY 6

CARRYING HOPE IN OUR HEARTS

To choose hope is to step firmly forward into the howling wind, baring one's chest to the elements, knowing that, in time, the storm will pass.

—Dalai Lama and Desmond Tutu,
The Book of Joy[32]

Life is such these days that the tendency to be discouraged grows steadily. Many wonder if a decrease in the amount of suffering is possible. Some suggest that people should forget about the big picture and just live their own life the best they can. Others prefer to back away entirely from thinking about suffering, hiding out in a nest of false security. Neither of these are places where hope and compassion reside.

Now is the time to lean into the truth that lives at the core of who we are, a truth that Hendrix College professor Jay Mc-Daniel names well: "The lure of God within each human life is not only a lure to live but also a lure to live well, to live with beauty—with harmony and intensity—relative to the situation at hand. In other words, the indwelling lure of God within each human life is not only an inner impulse to creatively adapt to new situations; it is also an impulse to seek the good, to be open to what is true, and to celebrate what is beautiful—all of which are forms of creative adaptation."[33]

If we fail to tend to the "lure of God" within us, the endless information about suffering on our planet saturates our spirit with discouragement. Joy, beauty, happiness, gratitude, understanding, and a sense of purpose and meaning—these await our reception if we turn in their direction. We lose hope if our only focus is on suffering. To retain energy and strength in expressing compassion day by day, we must have balance. One way I do this is by answering this question in my daily journal: "What do I want to remember from yesterday?" I am often surprised by the good I overlooked because I got caught in the not-so-good, missed some gesture of kindness when rushing to get something done, lost the melody of a lovely songbird when too preoccupied on my phone. We must be intentional about seeking what soothes our mind and restores our spirit, while at the same time being ever vigilant to how we can be compassionate.

Judy Lief, author of *Making Friends with Death*, notes how easy it is to fall into despair about our global situation: "When you feel your mind and heart filled to the point of claustrophobia with thoughts of disaster, fear and despair, it is good to bring to mind the many counter examples of human kindness and sanity, which are so easily overlooked. If you think about it, the degree in which our world is stitched together with loving-kindness is extraordinary."[34] We forget that genuine care resides among those with whom we share existence when we are constantly rushing around, lost in our to-do lists. The ways that people care then eludes us, and another source of hope gets smothered under the lid of nonawareness.

Gratefulness supports hope and generates compassion. The more aware I am of the benefits in my life, the more apt I am to be peaceful and loving. When I let go of comparison and competition, when I tell worry and fretting to be on their way,

I see more clearly what is wonder-full in and around me. My heart responds more lovingly when I approach suffering with peacefulness.

Tending to our personal transformation helps immensely to keep hope alive. As Etty Hillesum noted in her diary, "We have to take everything that comes: the bad with the good, which does not mean we cannot devote our life to curing the bad. But we must know what motives inspire our struggle, and we must begin with ourselves, every day anew."[35] "Beginning with my-self" means resting my compassionate action on the foundation of regular meditation and prayer.

Archbishop Desmond Tutu, truly a hope-filled person who believes that people are good, lives with a grateful heart. In spite of the struggles he witnessed in his own country, the death threats received, and the dreams dashed, this man of deep faith continues to trust in humanity. When discussing the topic of hope, Tutu remarked, "Yes, we do have setbacks, but you must keep everything in perspective. The world is getting better. Think about the rights of women or how slavery was considered morally justified a few hundred years ago. It takes time. We are growing and learning how to be compassionate, how to be caring, how to be human."[36] We can keep hope alive if we do not lose sight of that truth—we are "growing and learning" how to be compassionate. We are not finished products; we are human beings in process.

The morphogenic field of compassion grows stronger with every compassionate thought, word, and deed each of us generates. Our culture of instant everything, with a plethora of information at our fingertips, leads us to believe we ought to change difficult things quickly. However, significant social change rarely happens that way. Slowly, day by day, person by person, organization by organization, prayer by prayer, good deed after good deed, kindness after kindness, nonjudgmental thought after nonjudgmental thought—this is how a lessening of suffering occurs. We may not see it happening. That is where faith joins hands with trust. John Lewis writes, "Faith, to me, is knowing in the solid core of your soul that the work is already done, even as an idea is being conceived in your mind. It is being as sure as you are about your dreams as you are about anything you know as a hard fact. . . . Faith is being so sure of what the spirit has whispered in your heart that your belief in its eventuality is un-shakeable. . . . Even if you do not live to see it come to pass, you know without one doubt that it will be. That is faith."[37]

Judy Cannato's beautiful summary of the consequences of compassion contains an incentive to keep standing alongside suffering with a loving heart: "Compassion changes everything. Compassion heals. Compassion mends the broken and restores what has been lost. Compassion draws together those who have been estranged or never even dreamed they were connected. Compassion pulls us out of ourselves and into the heart of an-other, placing us on holy ground where we instinctively take off our shoes and walk in reverence. Compassion springs out of vulnerability and triumphs in unity."[38]

Let us have hope that this reality will come to pass.

REFLECTION

Where do you find hope in your life and in the life of our world?

PRAYER

"Lead me from death to life, from falsehood to truth. Lead me from despair to hope, from fear to trust. Lead me from hate to love, from war to peace. Let peace fill our heart, our world, our universe" (Satish Kumar, *Prayer for Peace*).

SCRIPTURE TO CARRY IN YOUR HEART TODAY

"Now faith is the assurance of things hoped for, the conviction of things not seen" (Heb 11:1).

WEEK 6, DAY 7

REVIEW AND REST

Our world is abundant with quiet, hidden lives of beauty and courage and goodness. There are millions of people at any given moment, young and old, giving themselves over to service, risking hope, and all the while ennobling us all. To take such goodness in and let it matter — to let it define our take on reality as much as headlines of violence — is a choice we can make to live by the light in the darkness, to be brave and free. . . . Taking in the good, whenever and wherever we find it, gives us new eyes for seeing and living.

—Krista Tippett, *Becoming Wise*[39]

Choose any or all of the following as a way to review Week Six:

- What three aspects of "Becoming a Compassionate Presence" were of greatest significance to you this past week?
- What would you name as the central characteristic of a "compassionate presence"?
- Which day's reflection challenged you the most?
- Which one left you nodding your head yes?

- Which of the six weeks most stimulated your interest and led you to want to be more compassionate in thought, word, and deed?

- How would you describe *Boundless Compassion*'s influence on your life amid a world where violence and poverty seem endless?

- Name the choices that you intend to make regarding the suffering of self and the suffering of all beings, both human and nonhuman.

- As you complete this last review, take a wide sweep over the past six weeks. Reflect on what you want to remember. Recall how you felt drawn at certain times toward a particular change in attitude or behavior. Conclude your review with your hands over your heart in a gesture of love for all of life. Bow in gratitude to the Holy One's guidance. Then hold your hands out in front of you once more and send your compassion forth into the world.

PILOGUE

I once heard a story about a small group of leaders who went searching for the Cave of Wisdom. Legend foretold that this place provided marvelous knowledge and guidance for those who located it. The explorers set out with hope of retrieving this perception and direction for their lives and for the people they served. The journey took a considerable amount of steady traveling, getting lost in the dark, asking directions, and plotting their way. The seekers traveled through all sorts of weather, stumbling at times along difficult terrain, but determined to find this treasured site.

Finally, their long-sought goal came into view. They breathed a sigh of joy as they arrived at the Cave of Wisdom, where they found a friendly guard at its entrance. The guard welcomed them heartily and invited them forward. But the leaders hesitated. They turned to converse among themselves. Then they replied to the guard, "Thank you, but we have no time for exploration. We just want to say we've been here." Having said this, they turned around and headed back to where they began.

Their response echoes a concern I have for those who read *Boundless Compassion*. The journey of compassion does not stop with the end of this book. It has only begun. So much waits to be discovered, explored, and integrated into daily living. Compassionate presence will always require taking another step further into personal transformation. This way of life is continually evolving.

The Guard at the door of your heart invites you to come into the "cave of compassion." I hope you will enter there often and find the treasures that await you.

ACKNOWLEDGMENTS

When I think of how this book has arrived in your hands, there immediately appears in my consciousness a lengthy list of people to whom I am indebted. Whether at an event or through an electronic message or another form of communication, I have been continually gifted with support for my endeavors, along with suggestions, stories, and resources from which I gleaned a clearer, fuller understanding of compassion. My gratitude overflows for the benefits I received from the following:

My colleagues and codirectors of Boundless Compassion: Margaret Stratman, O.S.M.; and Valeria Lewandoski, O.S.M. With their input, guidance, and support, we have shaped and evolved the focus and content of the Boundless Compassion programs into a valuable, transformational resource.

Directors and coordinators who welcomed me when I led the four-day Boundless Compassion conferences and retreats at their locations, including Maryknoll Institute in Maryknoll, New York; San Damiano in Danville, California; the Franciscan Renewal Center in Scottsdale, Arizona; the Spirit in the Desert Center in Carefree, Arizona; Sophia Spirituality Center in Atchison, Kansas; Wisdom Ways Spirituality Center in St. Paul, Minnesota; Siena Retreat Center in Racine, Wisconsin; Family Life

Center in St. Louis, Missouri; Mercy Center in Auckland, New Zealand; Dromantine Retreat Centre in Northern Ireland; Copper Beech Center in West Hartford, Connecticut; Servite Center of Compassion in Omaha, Nebraska; Sisters of St. Joseph Retreat Center in Wheeling, West Virginia; Bon Secours Spirituality Center in Marriottsville, Maryland; the Servite Sisters in the United Kingdom; and the Servite Priory in Benburb, Northern Ireland.

The videos of the four-day presentations could not have been made without the skills of cameraman, Rodger Routh, and the assistance of Amy Vollstedt, information technician at Sacred Heart School in West Des Moines, Iowa.

The generous people who suggested valuable resources from which I gleaned much-needed information and confirmation regarding how to live compassionately—while many names escape my remembrance, others I never knew. The information came as a title on a piece of paper slipped to me, a verbal response in a large group setting after a presentation, or a book left on the podium. Some I do recall and offer thanks: Kathi Bentall; Rose Mary Dougherty, S.S.N.D.; Maureen Conroy, R.S.M.; Marilyn Dodge; Nancy Flaherty; Linda Garcia; Tom Green; Rita Guariglia; Mary Jones; Robin Kline; Barbara Lund; David Manders; Joseph Nassal, C.PP.S.; Margaret Woodson Nea; Paddy O'Rourke, S.M.A.; John Pollard; Austin Repath; Edie Silvestri; Macrina Wiederkehr, O.S.B.; and Robert Wicks.

Artists Rita Loyd and Mary Southard, who generously allowed me use of their exquisite paintings depicting compassion.

The kind individuals whose homes and spirituality centers provided quiet space where I could write: Tim and Trudy Barry; Bill Walker; St. Benedict Center at Schuyler, Nebraska; Rivendell Center on Bowen Island, British Columbia; the Servants of Mary community in Omaha, Nebraska; and the Jesuit Retreat Center in Griswold, Iowa.

Those who pray for me daily—how I count on this and recognize the strength and energy that come to me because of this valued gift. I express gratitude especially to Janet Barnes, whose loving prayer has sustained my writing through the years.

The staff at Ave Maria Press. I am grateful for every mind, heart, and hand that brought this book to you. In particular I thank publisher Thomas Grady, marketing and sales director Karey Circosta, publicist Stephanie Sibal, and Jon Sweeney, who carefully sculpted my manuscript with his excellent editorial skills.

NOTES

INTRODUCTION

1. Donald P. McNeill, Douglas A. Morrison, and Henri J. M. Nouwen, *Compassion: A Reflection on the Christian Life* (New York: Image Books, 1983), 3–4.

2. Christina Feldman, *Compassion: Listening to the Cries of the World* (Berkeley, CA: Rodmell Press, 2005), 13.

3. Henri J. M. Nouwen, *A Spirituality of Caregiving*, edited by John S. Mogabgab (Nashville: Upper Room Books, 2011), 30.

4. Pope Francis, "Misericordiae Vultus," in *The Complete Encyclicals, Bulls, and Apostolic Exhortations*, vol. 1 (Notre Dame, IN: Ave Maria Press, 2016), 202.

5. Desmond Tutu and Mpho Tutu, *Made for Goodness* (New York: HarperOne, 2010), 5, 7.

WEEK ONE: COMPASSION AS A WAY OF LIFE

1. *Pastoral Constitution on the Church in the Modern World, Gaudium et Spes* ("Joy and Hope"), in *Documents of Vatican II*, vol. 1 (New York: America Press, 1966), preface 1, 199–200.

2. Paul Gilbert and Choden, *Mindful Compassion: How the Science of Compassion Can Help You Understand Your Emotions, Live in the Present, and Connect Deeply with Others* (Oakland, CA: New Harbinger, 2014), 1.

3. Norman Fischer, *Training in Compassion: Zen Teachings in the Practice of Lojong* (Boston: Shambhala, 2013), 55.

4. Matt Malone, S.J., "All the Way with J.F.K.," *America*, May 29, 2017, 3.

5. Ilia Delio, O.S.F., *Compassion: Living in the Spirit of St. Francis* (Cincinnati: Franciscan Media, 2011), xv.

6. Jessica Powers, "The Ledge of Light," in *The Selected Poetry of Jessica Powers*, edited by Regina Siegfried and Robert F. Morneau (Kansas City, MO: Sheed & Ward, 1989), 22.

7. Krista Tippett, *Becoming Wise: An Inquiry into the Mystery and Art of Living* (New York: Penguin, 2016), 111.

8. Lynne McTaggart, *The Bond: How to Fix Your Falling-Down World* (New York: Free Press, 2011), 4–7, 10–16.

9. *Gaudium et Spes*, preface 1, 199–200.

10. Carl Safina, *Beyond Words: What Animals Think and Feel* (New York: Henry Holt, 2015), 3.

11. Jack Kornfield, *The Wise Heart: A Guide to the Universal Teachings of Buddhist Psychology* (New York: Bantam Books, 2008), 296.

12. Gilbert and Choden, *Mindful Compassion*, 13.

13. Daniel Siegel, *Mindsight* (New York: Bantam Books, 2011), 39.

14. McTaggart, *The Bond*, 56.

15. Paul Gilbert, *The Compassionate Mind: A New Approach to Life's Challenges* (Oakland, CA: New Harbinger, 2009), 30.

16. Henri Nouwen, *The Way of the Heart*, cited in Henri Nouwen, *A Spirituality of Caregiving*, edited by John S. Mogabgab (Nashville: Upper Room Books, 2011), 19.

17. Joseph Nassal, C.PP.S., has often been a presenter for the Boundless Compassion programs.

18. George Smiga, "Beginning with Compassion," *Living with Christ*, July 2015, 16.

19. Rabbi Michael Paley, quoted in Kerry M. Olitzky and Lori Forman, *Sacred Intentions: Morning Inspiration to Strengthen the Spirit, Based on Jewish Wisdom* (Woodstock, VT: Jewish Lights Publishing, 1999), 359.

20. Christina Feldman, *Compassion: Listening to the Cries of the World* (Berkeley, CA: Rodmell Press, 2005), 4.

21. Marianne Williamson, *Illuminata: A Return to Prayer* (New York: Random House, 1994), 217.

22. Mahatma Gandhi, quoted at *BrainyQuote*, accessed August 9, 2017, https://www.brainyquote.com/quotes/authors/m/mahatma_gandhi.html.

23. Gwendolyn Brooks, "In Montgomery," in *In Montgomery: And Other Poems* (Chicago: Third World Press, 2003), 4.

24. Jean Vanier, *Encountering the Other* (Mahwah, NJ: Paulist Press, 2005), 57.

25. Jack Kornfield, *A Path with Heart: A Guide through the Perils and Promises of Spiritual Life* (New York: Bantam Books, 1993), 284–85.

26. Mark Nepo, *Seven Thousand Ways to Listen: Staying Close to What Is Sacred* (New York: Free Press, 2012), 114.

27. Dhyani Ywahoo, *Voices of Our Ancestors: Cherokee Teachings from the Wisdom Fire* (Boston: Shambhala, 1987), 177–78.

28. Thich Nhat Hanh, "Watering the Seeds of Happiness," *Shambhala Sun*, November 2014, 46.

29. Gilbert, *The Compassionate Mind*, 56.

30. Jon Kabat Zinn, *Wherever You Go, There You Are: Mindfulness Meditation in Daily Life* (New York: Hyperion Books, 1994), 17.

31. Gilbert, *The Compassionate Mind*, 180.

32. Cynthia Bourgeault, *Centering Prayer and Inner Awakening* (Cambridge, MA: Cowley Publications, 2004), 165.

33. Diane M. Millis, *Conversation—The Sacred Art: Practicing Presence in an Age of Distraction* (Woodstock, VT: SkyLight Paths Publishing, 2013), 103.

34. Delio, *Compassion*, 70.

WEEK TWO: WELCOMING OURSELVES

1. Christina Feldman, *Compassion: Listening to the Cries of the World* (Berkeley, CA: Rodmell Press, 2005), 84.

2. Sharon Salzberg, *The Force of Kindness: Change Your Life with Love and Compassion* (Boulder, CO: Sounds True, 2005), 18.

3. Kristin Neff, *Self-Compassion: Stop Beating Yourself Up and Leave Insecurity Behind* (New York: HarperCollins, 2011), 42.

4. Feldman, *Compassion*, 83–84.

5. Kabir Edmund Helminski gives this definition of abundant life: "The result of consciously becoming whole with mind, body, soul, and ecology." *Living Presence: A Sufi Way to Mindfulness and the Essential Self* (New York: Putnam Books, 1992), 176.

6. Gail Straub, *The Rhythm of Compassion: Caring for Self, Connecting with Society* (Boston: Tuttle, 2000), 60.

7. Straub, *Rhythm of Compassion*, 1–6, 60, 75, 89–90.

8. Pope Francis and Guiliano Vigini, *The Church of Mercy* (Chicago: Loyola Press, 2014), 17.

9. Wendi Steines, quoted in Andrew Solomon, *Far from the Tree: Parents, Children, and the Search for Identity* (New York: Scribner, 2012), 34.

10. Christopher K. Germer, *The Mindful Path to Self-Compassion: Freeing Yourself from Destructive Thoughts and Emotions* (New York: Guilford Press, 2009), 62–63.

11. Rita Loyd, *Unconditional Self-Love* (Madison, AL: Nurturing Art, 2010), 63.

12. Albert Nolan, *Jesus Today* (Maryknoll, NY: Orbis Books, 2006), 68.

13. The following passages all make reference to Jesus going apart for prayer and rest: Mt 14:23; Mk 1:35; Mk 6:46; Lk 3:21; Lk 5:16; Lk 6:12; Lk 9:18, 28; Jn 8:1.

14. Examples of the ways in which Jesus extended compassion toward himself include the following passages: Mt 12:14–21; Mk 14:32; Lk 5:1–3; Jn 2:1–11; Jn 4:6; Jn 11:33–40; Jn 12:1–7.

15. David Whyte, "Coleman's Bed," in *River Flow: New and Selected Poems* (Langley, WA: Many Rivers Press, 2007), 288.

16. Marianne Williamson, *A Return to Love: Reflections on the Principles of a Course in Miracles* (New York: HarperOne, 1992), 135.

17. Pema Chödrön, *Start Where You Are: A Guide to Compassionate Living* (Boston: Shambhala, 1994), 6.

18. Feldman, *Compassion*, 84.

19. Pema Chödrön, quoted in Andrea Miller, "Pema Chödrön on 4 Keys to Waking Up," *Shambhala Sun*, March

3, 2014, as found online at https://www.lionsroar.com/pema-chodron-on-4-keys-to-waking-up-march-2014/.

20. Parker Palmer, *Let Your Life Speak: Listening for the Voice of Vocation* (San Francisco: Jossey-Bass, 2000), 70–71.

21. Brené Brown, *The Gifts of Imperfection: Let Go of Who You Think You're Supposed to Be and Embrace Who You Are* (Center City, MN: Hazelden, 2010), 1.

22. James Martin, S.J., *James Martin, S.J.: Essential Writings*, edited by James T. Keane, (Maryknoll, NY: Orbis Books, 2017), 72.

23. William A. Miller, *Make Friends with Your Shadow: How to Accept and Use Positively the Negative Side of Your Personality* (Minneapolis: Augsburg, 1981), 114.

24. Robert J. Wicks, *Riding the Dragon: Ten Lessons for Inner Strength in Challenging Times* (Notre Dame, IN: Sorin Books, 2003), 46.

25. Francine Russo, "The Givers," *Scientific American Mind* (November–December 2016): 1.

26. Henri Nouwen, *A Spirituality of Caregiving*, 24.

27. Straub, *Rhythm of Compassion*, 59.

28. Caridade Drago, "Freed Speech," *America*, January 4–11, 2016, 29.

29. Neff, *Self-Compassion*, 1.

30. Dhyani Ywahoo, *Voices of Our Ancestors: Cherokee Teachings from the Wisdom Fire* (Boston: Shambhala, 1987), 46.

WEEK THREE: THE RIVER OF SUFFERING

1. St. John of the Cross, "River of Suffering," posted by Dan Burke, February 28, 2012, at http://www.spiritualdirection.com/2012/02/28/river-of-suffering-st-john-of-the-cross.

2. Francis Weller, *Entering the Healing Ground: Grief, Ritual and the Soul of the World* (Santa Rosa, CA: Wisdom Bridge Press, 2012), 27–64.

3. Francis Weller, *The Wild Edge of Sorrow: Rituals of Renewal and the Sacred Work of Grief* (Berkeley, CA: North Atlantic Books, 2015), 37.

4. Joan Chittister, *The Story of Ruth: Twelve Moments in Every Woman's Life* (Grand Rapids, MI: Wm. B. Eerdmans, 2000), 12.

5. Langston Hughes, "The Negro Speaks of Rivers," as found at https://www.poets.org/poetsorg/poem/negro-speaks-rivers.

6. Nouwen, McNeill, Morrison, *Compassion*, 25.

7. Barbara Brown Taylor, *God in Pain: Teaching Sermons on Suffering* (Nashville: Abingdon Press, 1998), 118.

8. Christina Feldman, *Compassion: Listening to the Cries of the World* (Berkeley, CA: Rodmell Press, 2005), 22.

9. Feldman, *Compassion*, 17–19.

10. Barbara Brown Taylor, *An Altar in the World: A Geography of Faith* (New York: HarperOne, 2009), 161.

11. Michael Himes, "The Suffering of Christ," *Suffering and the Christian Life*, edited by Richard W. Miller (Maryknoll, NY: Orbis Books, 2013), 122.

12. John O'Donohue, *Eternal Echoes: Exploring Our Hunger to Belong* (New York: Bantam Press, 1998), 161.

13. Dalai Lama, *An Open Heart* (New York: Little, Brown and Co., 2001), 91.

14. Karla McLaren, *The Art of Empathy: A Complete Guide to Life's Most Essential Skill* (Boulder, CO: Sounds True, 2013), 4.

15. Ilia Delio, O.S.F., *Compassion: Living in the Spirit of St. Francis* (Cincinnati: Franciscan Media, 2011), 47.

16. McNeill, Morrison, and Nouwen, *Compassion*, 15.

17. Raymond Barfield, interviewed in Janice Lynch Schuster, "The Miracle in Front of You," *The Sun*, January 2016, 10.

18. Mother Teresa, *A Call to Mercy: Hearts to Love, Hands to Serve*, edited by Brian Kolodiejchuk, M.C. (New York: Image, 2016), 49.

19. Levi Coffin's story is found online at https://en.wikipedia.org/wiki/Levi_Coffin.

20. "Letters to Editor," *The Sun*, December 2016, 3.

21. Rachel Naomi Remen, *Kitchen Table Wisdom* (New York: Riverhead Books, 1996), 161.

22. Edward Foley, O.F.M. Cap., "Last Supper Tuesday?" *Give Us This Day*, April 11, 2017, 143.

23. Mark Nepo, *Seven Thousand Ways to Listen: Staying Close to What Is Sacred* (New York: Free Press, 2012), 144.

24. Information on Literacy Volunteers on the Green can be found at http://www.lvg-ct.org.

25. Joseph Nassal, C.PP.S., *The Conspiracy of Compassion* (Leavenworth, KS: Forest of Peace Publishing, 1997), 49.

26. Joanna Macy, *World as Lover, World as Self* (Berkeley, CA: Parallax Press, 1991), 187.

27. Parker Palmer, *Healing the Heart of Democracy* (San Francisco: Jossey-Bass, 2011), 60.

28. Bryan Stevenson, *Just Mercy: A Story of Justice and Redemption* (New York: Spiegel & Grau, 2014), 306–8.

29. Naomi Shihab Nye, "Kindness," in *Words under the Words: Selected Poems* (Portland, OR: Far Corner Books, 1995), 42–43.

30. St. John of the Cross, *John of the Cross: Selected Writings*, edited by Kieran Kavanaugh (Mahwah, NJ: Paulist Press, 1987), 21.

31. Jack Kornfield, *A Lamp in the Darkness: Illuminating the Path through Difficult Times* (Boulder, CO: Sounds True, 2011), 49.

32. Kathleen Dowling Singh, *The Grace in Dying: How We Are Transformed Spiritually as We Die* (New York: HarperOne, 2000), 105.

33. James E. Miller and Susan C. Cutshall, *The Art of Being a Healing Presence: A Guide for Those in Caring Relationships* (Fort Wayne, IN: Willowgreen, 2001), 37.

34. Joseph Chilton Pearce, *The Biology of Transcendence: A Blueprint of the Human Spirit* (Rochester, VT: Park Street Press 2002), 56.

35. Rabbi Rami Shapiro, *The Sacred Art of Lovingkindness* (Woodstock, VT: Skylight Paths, 2006), 22.

36. Elizabeth Johnson, "Sacred Ground at the Bedside," in *Abounding in Kindness* (Maryknoll, NY: Orbis Books, 2015), 151.

37. Gail Straub, *The Rhythm of Compassion: Caring for Self, Connecting with Society* (Boston: Tuttle, 2000), 103.

38. Straub, *Rhythm of Compassion*, 95–97.

39. Straub, *Rhythm of Compassion*, 97.

40. Straub, *Rhythm of Compassion*, 97, 103.

41. Straub, *Rhythm of Compassion*, 97.

42. Ram Dass with Rameshwar Das, *Polishing the Mirror: How to Live from Your Spiritual Heart* (Boulder, CO: Sounds True, 2013), 109.

WEEK FOUR: FROM HOSTILITY TO HOSPITALITY

1. Robert Lentz and Edwina Gateley, *Christ in the Margins* (Maryknoll, NY: Orbis Books, 2009), 7.

2. John Lewis, *Across That Bridge: Life Lessons and a Vision for Change* (New York: Hyperion Books, 2012), 96–98.

3. Vatican II, "Message to Humanity," in *Pastoral Constitution on the Church in the Modern World, Gaudium et Spes* ("Joy and Hope"), in *Documents of Vatican II*, vol. 1 (New York: America Press, 1966), 5.

4. Henri J. M. Nouwen, *Reaching Out: The Three Movements of the Spiritual Life* (New York: Doubleday, 1975), 65.

5. Jim Wallis, "Robin Hood in Reverse," *Sojourners*, April 2017, 7.

6. Hosffman Ospino, "What Did You Call Me?" *Give Us This Day*, January 14, 2017, 144.

7. Thomas Kelly, *A Testament of Devotion* (New York: Harper-Collins, 1941), 74–75.

8. Pope Francis, *Morning Homilies III* (Maryknoll, NY: Orbis Books, 2016), 114.

9. Rick Hanson, *Buddha's Brain: The Practical Neuroscience of Happiness, Love and Wisdom* (Oakland, CA: New Harbinger, 2009), 133.

10. Hanson, *Buddha's Brain*, 121.

11. Hanson, *Buddha's Brain*, 132–33.

12. Hanson, *Buddha's Brain*, 133.

13. Jerome Kodell, O.S.B., "The Good Fight," *America*, April 25, 2011, 15.

14. Edwina Gateley, *A Mystical Heart: 52 Weeks in the Presence of God* (New York: Crossroad Publishing, 1998), 94–95.

15. Vandana Shiva, *Earth Democracy: Justice, Sustainability, and Peace* (Cambridge, MA: South End Press, 2005), 117.

16. Andrew Solomon, *Far from the Tree: Parents, Children and the Search for Identity* (New York: Scribner, 2012), 5, 95, 121.

17. Jean Vanier, *Jean Vanier: Essential Writings*, edited by Carolyn Whitney-Brown (Maryknoll, NY: Orbis Books, 2008), 53.

18. "A Credo for Support," YouTube video, posted by Norman Kunc, October 16, 2006, https://www.youtube.com/watch?v=wunHDfZFxXw.

19. Bryan Stevenson, *Just Mercy: A Story of Justice and Redemption* (New York: Spiegel & Grau, 2014), 148–51, 161–62.

20. Lewis, *Across That Bridge*, 173–74.

21. Jean Vanier, quoted in Krista Tippett, *Becoming Wise: An Inquiry into the Mystery and Art of Living* (New York: Penguin, 2016), 83–84.

22. Ilia Delio, O.S.F., *Compassion: Living in the Spirit of St. Francis* (Cincinnati: Franciscan Media, 2011), 58.

23. Maureen O'Connell, *Compassion: Loving Our Neighbor in an Age of Globalization* (Maryknoll, NY: Orbis Books, 2009), 90.

24. O'Connell, *Compassion*, 19.

25. O'Connell, *Compassion*, 7, 20.

26. John Heagle, *Justice Rising: The Emerging Biblical Vision* (Maryknoll, NY: Orbis Books, 2010), 43, 49.

27. Heagle, *Justice Rising*, 45–46.

28. Heagle, *Justice Rising*, 50.

29. Jean Vanier, Templeton Award Speech, 2015, available at YouTube, posted by "TempletonPrize," March 11, 2015, https://www.youtube.com/watch?v=dEgQLo2HBV4.

30. Marilyn Lacey, R.S., *This Flowing toward Me* (Notre Dame, IN: Ave Maria Press, 2009), 182.

31. Wangari Maathai, *Unbowed: A Memoir* (NY: Random House, 2006), 130–38.

32. St. John of the Cross, quoted in *Evelyn Underhill: Essential Writings*, edited by Emilie Griffin (Maryknoll, NY: Orbis Books, 2003), 58.

33. Mother Teresa, *A Call to Mercy: Hearts to Love, Hands to Serve*, edited by Brian Kolodiejchuk, M.C. (New York: Image, 2016), 3.

34. Dorothy Day, *Dorothy Day: Selected Writings*, edited by Robert Ellsberg (Maryknoll, NY: Orbis Books, 2001), 94, 96.

35. Jean Vanier, *Encountering the Other* (Mahwah, NJ: Paulist Press, 2005), 60–61.

36. Pope Francis and Guiliano Vigini, *The Church of Mercy* (Chicago: Loyola Press, 2014), 31.

WEEK FIVE: A THOUSAND UNBREAKABLE LINKS

1. Angeles Arrien, *The Four-Fold Way* (San Francisco: HarperSanFrancisco, 1993), 6.

2. Jane Goodall, interviewed in "How to Be a Bodhisattva," *Shambhala Sun*, July 2013, 22.

3. Mary Oliver, *Upstream* (New York: Penguin, 2016), 154.

4. Andrew Harvey, *The Way of Passion* (Berkeley, CA: North Atlantic Books, 1994), 56.

5. Elizabeth A. Johnson, *Ask the Beasts: Darwin and the God of Love* (New York: Bloomsbury, 2015), 5.

6. Mary Southard's art can be viewed at http://www.mary-southardart.org.

7. Neil deGrasse Tyson, quoted at *BrainyQuote*, accessed August 9, 2017, https://www.brainyquote.com/quotes/quotes/n/neildegras531166.html.

8. Sally Ride, as quoted in "The Writer's Almanac," National Public Radio, May 26, 2014.

9. Judy Cannato, *Radical Amazement: Contemplative Lessons from Black Holes, Supernovas, and Other Wonders of the Universe* (Notre Dame, IN: Sorin Books, 2006), 32.

10. Joanna Macy, John Seed, Pat Fleming, and Arne Naess, *Thinking like a Mountain: Towards a Council of All Beings* (Santa Cruz, CA: New Society Publications, 1998), 9.

11. Faith Shearin, "My Daughter Describes the Tarantula," *Telling the Bees* (Nacogdoches, TX: Stephen F. Austin State University Press, 2015), as quoted in "The Writer's Almanac," National Public Radio, June 21, 2015.

12. Carl Safina, *Beyond Words: What Animals Think and Feel* (New York: Henry Holt, 2015), 53–65.

13. Peter Wohlleben, *The Hidden Life of Trees: What They Feel, How They Communicate* (Berkeley, CA: Greystone Books, 2015), 15–16.

14. Wohlleben, *Hidden Life of Trees*, 8–9.

15. Cannato, *Radical Amazement*, 57.

16. Johnson, *Ask the Beasts*, xvii.

17. Pope Francis, *On Care for Our Common Home, Laudato Si'* (Washington, DC: United States Conference of Catholic Bishops, 2015), no. 161, p. 78.

18. Letitia L. Star, "The Year to Go Zero Waste," *Spirituality and Health* (January–February 2017): 80–81.

19. Ajahn Brahm, *Who Ordered This Truckload of Dung? Inspiring Stories for Welcoming Life's Difficulties* (Somerville, MA: Wisdom Publications, 2005), 135–36.

20. Pope Francis, *Laudato Si'*, no. 11, pp. 5–6.

21. Thomas Berry, *The Great Work: Our Way into the Future* (New York: Bell Tower, 1999), 17.

22. Pierre Teilhard de Chardin, *Pierre Teilhard de Chardin: Writings*, edited by Ursula King (Maryknoll, NY: Orbis Books, 1999), 27.

23. Berry, *Great Work*, 17.

24. John Luma, "When Nature Is Nurture," *Newsweek*, February 11, 2008, 20.

25. Br. Lawrence of the Resurrection, *The Practice of the Presence of God* (Springfield, IL: Templegate, 1974), 29.

26. Macrina Wiederkehr, *Gold in Your Memories* (Notre Dame, IN: Ave Maria Press, 1998), 16.

27. Sally McFague, *The Body of God: An Ecological Theology* (Minneapolis: Augsburg Fortress Press, 1993), 211.

28. Jane Goodall, in Donald Altman's *Meal by Meal: 365 Daily Meditations for Finding Balance through Mindful Eating* (Novato, CA: New World Library, 2004), May 16.

29. John O'Donohue, *Anam Cara: A Book of Celtic Wisdom* (New York: Bantam Press, 1998), 87.

30. Macy, et al., *Thinking like a Mountain*.

31. Vandana Shiva, *Earth Democracy: Justice, Sustainability, and Peace* (Cambridge, MA: South End Press, 2005), 145.

32. Linda Lear, *Rachel Carson: Witness for Nature* (New York: Henry Holt, 1997), 428–56.

33. Goodall interview, *Shambhala Sun*, July 2013, 22.

34. Shiva, *Earth Democracy*, 145.

35. Pope Francis, *Laudato Si'*, nos. 164, 92, pp. 80, 45.

36. Ilia Delio, *The Emergent Christ: Exploring the Meaning of Catholic in an Evolutionary Universe* (Maryknoll, NY: Orbis Books, 2011), 10.

37. Jan L. Richardson, *Sacred Journeys: A Woman's Book of Daily Prayer* (Nashville: Upper Room Books, 1996), 15.

38. Pierre Teilhard de Chardin, *Pierre Teilhard de Chardin: Writings*, edited by Ursula King (Maryknoll, NY: Orbis Books, 1999), 27.

WEEK SIX: BECOMING A COMPASSIONATE PRESENCE

1. Harriet Tubman, quoted at *BrainyQuote*, accessed August 9, 2017, www.brainyquote.com.

2. Thomas Kelly, *A Testament of Devotion* (New York: Harper-Collins, 1941), 80–81.

3. Krista Tippett, *Becoming Wise: An Inquiry into the Mystery and Art of Living* (New York: Penguin, 2016), 176; quoted by Shaine Claiborne in an interview with Krista Tippett.

4. Carrie Newcomer, interviewed in "The Good News That Still Abides," *Sojourners*, January 2017, 43.

5. Macrina Wiederkehr, *Abide: Keeping Vigil with the Word of God* (Collegeville, MN: Liturgical Press, 2011), 49.

6. Marie Therese Archambault, *A Retreat with Black Elk: Living in the Sacred Hoop* (Cincinnati: St. Anthony Messenger Press, 1998), 25. See also Dhyani Ywahoo, *Voices of Our Ancestors: Cherokee Teachings from the Wisdom Fire* (Boston: Shambhala, 1987), 17, 57.

7. Harry Palmer, quoted at *The Light Party*, accessed August 9, 2017, http://lightparty.com/Peace/COMPASSI.html.

8. Charter for Compassion, accessed August 9, 2017, https://www.charterforcompassion.org/charter.

9. Gail Straub, *The Rhythm of Compassion: Caring for Self, Connecting with Society* (Boston: Tuttle, 2000), 169.

10. Henri Nouwen, *With Open Hands* (Notre Dame, IN: Ave Maria Press, 1972), 92.

11. Dalai Lama and Desmond Tutu, with Douglas Abrams, *The Book of Joy: Lasting Happiness in a Changing World* (New York: Penguin Random House, 2016), 142.

12. Etty Hillesum, *An Interupted Life, Etty Hillesum: An Interrupted Life, 1941–43, and Letters from Westerbork* (New York: Picador, 1996), 213.

13. Paula D'Arcy, *Stars at Night* (Cincinnati: Franciscan Media, 2016), 69.

14. Judy Cannato, *Field of Compassion: How the New Cosmology Is Transforming Spiritual Life* (Notre Dame, IN: Sorin Books, 2010), 27–30.

15. Cannato, *Field of Compassion*, 27.

16. Cannato, *Field of Compassion*, 6–7.

17. Christopher K. Germer, *The Mindful Path to Self-Compassion: Freeing Yourself from Destructive Thoughts and Emotions* (New York: Guilford Press, 2009), 165.

18. Dorothy Day, *Dorothy Day: Selected Writings*, edited by Robert Ellsberg (Maryknoll, NY: Orbis Books, 2001), 340.

19. Sisters of Notre Dame de Namur, *Martyr of the Amazon: The Life of Sister Dorothy Stang* (Maryknoll, NY: Orbis Books, 2005).

20. Gregory Boyle, *Tattoos on the Heart: The Power of Boundless Compassion* (New York: Free Press, 2010).

21. Kevin Hardy, "'Home Is What You Make It': Voices from the Anti-Pipeline Camp," *Des Moines Register*, December 11, 2016, 6A.

22. Thomas Merton, *New Seeds of Contemplation* (New York: New Directions, 2007), 250.

23. Jack Kornfield, *A Path with Heart: A Guide through the Perils and Promises of Spiritual Life* (New York: Bantam Books, 1993), 14.

24. Kornfield, *A Path with Heart*, 13.

25. Tracy Kidder, *Strength in What Remains: A Journey of Remembrance and Forgiveness* (New York: Random House, 2009).

26. Margaret Silf, "The Power of One," *America*, July 6, 2009.

27. Sr. Simone Campbell, quoted in Krista Tippett, *Becoming Wise: An Inquiry into the Mystery and Art of Living* (New York: Penguin, 2016), 128.

28. Howard Zinn, "The Optimism of Uncertainty," *The Sun*, October 2016, 25.

29. Hillesum, *An Interrupted Life*, 63.

30. China Galland, *The Bond between Women: A Journey to Fierce Compassion* (New York: Riverhead, 1998), 143.

31. Elizabeth Kübler-Ross, quoted at *Positive Outlooks Blog*, accessed August 9, 2017, https://postiveoutlooksblog.com.

32. Dalai Lama and Desmond Tutu, *The Book of Joy*, 122.

33. Jay McDaniel, *Gandhi's Hope* (Maryknoll, NY: Orbis Books, 2005), 94.

34. Judy Lief, "How Not to Freak Out," *Lion's Roar*, November 2016, 50.

35. Hillesum, *An Interrupted Life*, 154–55.

36. Dalai Lama and Desmond Tutu, *The Book of Joy*, 117.

37. John Lewis, *Across That Bridge: Life Lessons and a Vision for Change* (New York: Hyperion Books, 2012), 19–20.

38. Cannato, *Field of Compassion*, 8.

39. Tippett, *Becoming Wise*, 265.

Joyce Rupp is well known for her work as a writer, spiritual midwife, international retreat leader, and conference speaker. She is the author of numerous bestselling books, including *Praying Our Goodbyes*, *Open the Door*, and *Fragments of Your Ancient Name*. *Fly While You Still Have Wings* earned an award in the spirituality books category from the Catholic Press Association. Rupp is a member of the Servite (Servants of Mary) community and the codirector of the Servite Center of Compassion's Boundless Compassion program. She lives in West Des Moines, Iowa.

www.joycerupp.com
Facebook: joycerupp

Servite Center of Compassion:
www.osms.org/servite-center-of-compassion

ALSO AVAILABLE

PRAYER BOOK

Compassion was the center of Jesus' ministry and his mission for his disciples—and for us. Bestselling and award-winning author and retreat leader Joyce Rupp gives you the words to develop compassion in yourself as never before and to reenergize your ability to offer loving kindness to those around you.

Available from Ave Maria Press or wherever books and e-books are sold.

DVD Set

Also available is a set of five DVDs, each one containing an hour-long presentation by Joyce Rupp about one of the topics covered in *Boundless Compassion*. These teachings are a valuable resource for personal use, for small-group study, or for leading retreats and conferences on the subject of compassion.

These DVDs can be purchased from the www.osms.org gift shop or from www.joycerupp.com.